# NED KELLY
## Man and Myth

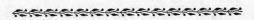

# Ned Kelly

## *Man and Myth*

*Edited with an Introduction by*
*Colin F. Cave,* B.A., B.ED., M.A.C.E.,
*Executive Director,*
*Adult Education Centre, Wangaratta*

Cassell Australia

Cassell Australia Limited
44 Waterloo Road, North Ryde, New South Wales 2113
30 Curzon Street, North Melbourne, Victoria 3051
in association with Cassell Limited, Auckland

First published 1968
Reprinted 1980
Cover design by Steven Dunbar
Set in 11/12 Baskerville
Printed and bound by Hedges & Bell Pty. Ltd., Maryborough, Vic.

National Library of Australia
Cataloguing-in-Publication Data

Ned Kelly: man and myth

2nd ed.
index
bibliography
ISBN 0 7269 1410 X

1. Kelly, Ned, 1855-1880
2. Bush — rangers — Biography

364.1'55'0924

# Contents

# Foreword

When this book was first published in 1968 the papers
and the discussion on those papers at the seminar on Ned
Kelly at Wangaratta during the Easter of the preceding
year presented a useful summary of the state of play on
two important subjects in the history of Australia — the
life of Ned Kelly and the reasons why he became a part of
the Australian conscience. Since that memorable and
lively exchange of opinions and ideas at the Wangaratta
seminar, deep in the heart of Kelly country, academics,
writers and artists have continued their sport with sport.
Now one hundred years after Ned's execution at the old
Melbourne gaol in 1880 Kellyana promises to become
quite an industry. Books will appear this year which will
sort out the facts in the life of Ned Kelly: books will
appear which will give a more profound explanation of
why a bushranger became a folk hero in Australia. No
one will ever put an end to our interest in our sport with
Ned, because he is part of all of us. That is why it is useful
to keep this collections of papers in print. It represents a
landmark in the people's discovery both about Ned and
therefore about themselves.

MANNING CLARK
*April 1980*

# Introduction

Australian history bears ample evidence of the high adventurous spirit of such men as Burke and Wills, Leichhardt, Strzelecki, Wentworth, Blaxland and Lawson, Cook and Flinders, Peter Lalor and a host of other memorable individuals who could well stand as symbols of human endeavour and courage. Such men are the folk heroes of which every country has need and around whom its legends are built.

And yet, the Australian legend, fashioned and sustained by the people, favours as its national hero, a bearded, braggart, brawling Irishman; horse-thief, bank-robber, bushranger and murderer; the loud-mouthed, law-breaking, swaggering son of an Irish convict, Ned Kelly — who spent most of his life being warned, hunted or jailed by the Law, and ended up twitching for four minutes from the end of the hangman's rope in Old Melbourne Jail; whose skull, it is said, was used as a paperweight by a minor public servant!

Some explanation of why this 'raw, bony man', this 'sallow-complexioned criminal' with the 'beard and moustache of a dirty dark red colour' should have assumed such heroic proportions is attempted in these pages. What is remarkable is that the Kelly reputation is founded on exploits covering a mere two years. And even more remarkable is that, whilst the Euroa and Jerilderie episodes may smack of that bold rascality which seems expected of legendary heroes, those at Stringybark Creek and Glenrowan may well give us pause and leave the mind open to serious doubts and fears.

How right are the respectable, the proper, to protest that this 'madman clad in iron' should not be idolized, pedestalled, almost beatified? How right to protest against the glorification of mere criminality in an age of growing defiance of the law? Even Robin Hood (to whom many liken Ned Kelly in an endeavour to rationalize his sins) appears at least to have been public-spirited; aiming his shafts at oppressive kings and bullying sheriffs, robbing the overbearing rich to help the suffering poor. By comparison Kelly appears no more than a scoundrel, robbing and eventually killing merely as a criminal. Yet, all in all, he had the earmarks of a popular hero — his exploits destined to form a basic component of the Australian *mystique*.

Probably born in December 1854, at Beveridge, about twenty-five miles north of Melbourne on what is now the Hume Highway, Edward Kelly was the eldest son and third child of an Irish ex-convict, John 'Red' Kelly, and an Irish migrant, Ellen Quinn — with whom he had eloped. For the most part of their adult lives, the Kellys and the Quinns (and their near relatives, the Lloyds) were in and out of court-houses and prisons.

As the eldest son, Ned Kelly had, at an early age, frequently to fend for his whole family, particularly his younger brother and his mother, whom he idolized. He resorted to various kinds of petty theft and law-breaking. He was warned by the police.

At the age of about twelve, he arrived with his family at Eleven Mile Creek, near Greta, in north-eastern Victoria; a wild, wooded, violent, uncompromising district in those days, nearly a hundred and fifty miles from Melbourne, the centre of law and order. When only a teenager, he was charged with robbery with violence against a Chinaman. The charge was dismissed. In the following year, he was charged with robbery under arms as the accomplice of Harry Power, a mountainous and notorious bushranger of the district. Again, the charge was dismissed, although there is little doubt of Kelly's complicity.

Later in the same year he was sentenced to six months (three with hard labour) in Beechworth Prison for assault and indecent behaviour against one Jeremiah McCormack and his wife. Kelly had knocked McCormack down in an argument over a horse; and was later charged with having had delivered to Mrs McCormack a parcel of calves' testicles with an obscene note.

A few months after his release, he was charged with receiving a stolen horse of one Isiah 'Wild' Wright. He was sentenced to three years, much of which he spent in Pentridge Jail in Melbourne and a prison hulk in Port Phillip Bay, as Beechworth Prison was not thought sufficiently tough for him.

After this spell, he lived what appeared to be a fairly respectable life for three years as a timber-cutter, station-hand and mill foreman in and around the Wombat Ranges — which were later to be his home in more difficult circumstances.

In 1877 (when he was in his early twenties) he was arrested for drunkenness and charged with resisting arrest after a wild and desperate fight with four policemen in a boot-maker's shop in Benalla on his way to the court. Despite police protests that he should be jailed, the magistrate only fined him.

A year later, in 1878, began the extraordinary sequence of events which finally led to the Long Drop. One can only thank the writers of the ensuing chapters for trying to make some sense out of the Fitzpatrick episode.

Constable Fitzpatrick, one of the four with whom Kelly had fought (later to be dismissed from the Force as a 'liar and a larrikin') was put in charge of the Greta police station on 15 April 1878. Determined to make an impression and to 'fix the Greta Mob', he visited the Kelly homestead at Eleven Mile Creek. Some time later, he staggered back to Benalla with the story that he had been assaulted and shot in the wrist by Ned Kelly after an altercation over horse-stealing. No one knows the truth of the story. Sufficient that Mrs Kelly, Ned's mother, who had apparently struck Fitzpatrick over the head with a shovel or a broom, was jailed for three years.

Ned Kelly, virtually outlawed, with a price on his head, and 'mad with rage' at the treatment of his mother, took to the hills — the Wombat Ranges — with his younger brother Dan, and two friends, Joe Byrne and Steve Hart. They were all fine bushmen, expert horsemen, and crack rifle shots.

Six months later, on 26 October 1878, Ned Kelly shot to death three policemen of a party of four sent into the Ranges to bring him in. Lonigan (whom Kelly had hated since the fight in Benalla), Scanlon and Kennedy — all Irishmen — lay dead in the Wombat Ranges, whilst Constable McIntyre, also of the search party, was allowed to go free. Again, the truth of the story is concealed and confused. McIntyre's evidence featured strongly in the trial of Kelly which is examined in detail in a later chapter.

Six weeks later, the four, known as by now the 'Kelly Gang', rode calmly into Euroa, Victoria, from a nearby station which they had taken over for the time being, and robbed the National Bank of £2,000. It was a sudden, but well planned, rather comradely affair, which did much to enhance the Kelly reputation. Then, only two months after this, the Kelly Gang skirted round the police guard on the New South Wales border, rode into the small township of Jerilderie, locked up the police in their own police station, donned their uniforms, escorted the wife of the police sergeant to church, spent two days of leisurely living, then held up the whole town and robbed the Bank of New South Wales of £2,000. It is possible that the police force did not recover for many years from this loss of face. The Kellys rode out on a wave of sympathetic admiration.

In June, 1880, Joe Byrne, now inextricably woven into the web of the Kelly story, shot to death his best friend, Aaron Sherritt, in his home at the Woolshed, near Beechworth, in the presence of Sherritt's wife and mother-in-law

4

and four policemen. The story of Aaron Sherritt is remarkable; and Ian Jones's paper in this book reveals Sherritt as
something less than the black-hearted villain and police
informer that he appears in many of the accounts of the
Kelly saga. It is quite probable that the life of Aaron
Sherritt (whom Joe Byrne believed to be an informer) was
sacrificed for the main purpose, not of silencing him, but of
initiating a carefully planned *coup de grâce* against the
police.

The events leading to the final débâcle at Glenrowan
happened with great speed. After Sherritt's cold-blooded
murder, Joe Byrne and Dan Kelly joined Ned and Steve
Hart in Glenrowan, a small wayside station near Greta,
between Wangaratta and Benalla, on the main railway line.
The four took over the town, leaving the Melbourne police
to believe that the gang was in or around Beechworth,
some miles away, where Sherritt had been shot. Some sixty
of the townspeople, many of them Kelly sympathizers, were
bailed up in Mrs Jones's Glenrowan Inn, where a festive
time was had by all. In the meantime, Ned had organized
the tearing up of the railway track so that the police train,
hurrying through Glenrowan on its way to Beechworth,
would plunge down a nearby ravine. However, the train
driver was warned by a schoolteacher, Thomas Curnow,
whom Kelly had allowed to leave the inn to 'tend his wife'.

Thus ensued the famous Siege of Glenrowan, which was
waged between the police and the Kelly Gang all the
morning and most of the afternoon of that Monday, 28
June 1880. Accounts are naturally confused. However, it
is certain that Joe Byrne was shot in the groin and died
soon after; that Ned Kelly left the Inn during the fighting
and some time later returned; that some civilians, including a small child, were shot; that Ned Kelly appeared before the whole battery of the police clad in his armour
made from ploughshares and challenged the lot of them;
that he was shot down through his unprotected legs, and
captured; that the police set fire to the inn, and the shock-

5

ingly burnt bodies of two men believed to be Dan Kelly and Steve Hart were later dragged from the ashes of the Inn and placed on public display.

Ned Kelly, wounded twenty-eight times, they say, but still living, was taken to Beechworth and thence to Melbourne Jail, where he was carefully nursed back to health to face trial. On 31 July 1880 he was taken back to Beechworth by train. At this preliminary hearing, he was committed to trial at the Beechworth Criminal Court but, in view of local high feeling, the trial was transferred to Melbourne.

The trial of Ned Kelly began in the Central Criminal Court, Melbourne, on 28 October 1880, before Judge Sir Redmond Barry, who two years previously had sentenced Mrs Kelly to prison in Beechworth for the assault on Fitzpatrick (the event, many believe, which sparked off all the later crimes). Kelly was found guilty of the murder of Constable Lonigan at Stringybark Creek and, after one of the most extraordinary exchanges between judge and prisoner ever recorded in legal history, Judge Barry sentenced Kelly to death.

Execution by hanging was carried out on the twenty-five-year-old Edward Kelly on 11 November 1880, Melbourne Cup Day.

These are the bare facts of the case. They are clothed in a great variety of facts, half-truths, lies, legends, memories, beliefs and opinions. A whole library of stories and anecdotes exists, most of them romantic, many of them no doubt true.

Kelly had a reputation for gentleness and trust in his fellow-men. He trusted Constable McIntyre; he trusted Aaron Sherritt; he trusted Thomas Curnow. They let him down. He was supposed to have saved a child from drowning in his early youth. He was almost always kind to women, gentlemanly and courteous. He had the traditional Irish charm. He also shot the defenceless Kennedy dead.

Much is made of Kelly's love of his mother and his indignation at her treatment by the police, of his family responsibilities when his father died, of his bringing up of his brother Dan, and of the fact that he had to steal to keep his family alive, not to mention that he had also to steal to provide his sympathizers with arms and armour.

There is the story of Kelly holding up a dance around Cooma way, where he took all the money, watches and jewellery of those present save that of a brave woman who 'treated him like a human being'. There is the story of Steve Hart fooling the police by racing around the countryside dressed as Kate Kelly, who was a fine horsewoman. There is the story of Kelly being dragged by a policeman across a street in Benalla by the private parts. There is the story that Ned's apparent drunkenness in Benalla was, in fact, the result of his being drugged by the police. There is the story of Ned forcing Steve Hart to return a stolen watch. There are innumerable stories of Ned's nocturnal visits to homesteads in the district where his charm and courtesy won all hearts. There is, on the other hand, the story of the dastard Fitzpatrick, and his association with Kate Kelly whom, some say, he got with child. There is the story of Ned Kelly's attempt to establish a republic.

People speak of his poetic qualities. They speak of his *camaraderie* in the Glenrowan Inn (waiting for a trainload of policemen to die). They speak of his fairness and sportsmanship at Stringybark Creek where he ordered the police to bail up when he could have shot them down in cold blood. When he could, perhaps, have ridden away from it all. They speak of the general admiration of the police and local people alike for his boldness and manly qualities. They speak of his universal kindness, courtesy, and chivalry toward women.

There are a host of stories, nearly all aimed at painting Ned Kelly as a gentleman — misunderstood, hounded into outlawry, fighting against insuperable odds, heroic in a battle to free his downtrodden people, a victim of his social circumstances; aimed at minimizing, rationalizing — merely disguising his crimes.

All this splendid, fiery, tragic, mad, criminal action is played against the backdrop of the 1870s; raw times, and times of conflict — the conflict of the little land-holder with economic depression, bad seasons, ruined crops, graft in high places; eking out a meagre living from the resentful and unyielding soil in a wild and lonely country: the conflict of the struggling free-selector with the hard-fisted, politically strong squatters: the conflict of the rebellious and disillusioned Irish not merely with conditions in Australia (that were very like those they had escaped from in Ireland) but with the hated British who ruled, held the land, and enforced the law: the more personal conflict of the Catholic Irish Kellys with the vindictive, swaggering 'jackals' of law and order.

They were indeed hard times in a hard country, times of despair, disillusionment, loneliness and hardship that are perhaps difficult for us to conceive. They were times when the young grew rough and reckless, and rode swift and brave and flash through bush and country streets alike.

The warp of hard cold facts of the Kellys' fight against law and order is coloured and patterned by the woof of hardship and overwhelming odds. And this is the stuff of the Kelly legend, the stuff from which heroes are cut. There are a hundred woven threads of this story to capture the imagination.

Glenrowan itself was a theatrical masterpiece of which Tyrone Guthrie, Peter Brook or even Cecil B. De Mille himself might well have been envious. It opens like a Ford Western, with the bold ride into town, the Gang brash and unafraid. There follows the roistering, tavernous wait in the Glenrowan Inn. Who could object to such behaviour? Who, indeed, would not like to be able to be so lawless with the same swagger and the same impunity? And then there is the Siege, with the brave quartet fighting it out; Kelly appearing like some latterday Achilles, clad in his awesome armour, challenging (in the recognized tradition of Jack Doolan) the whole of the asembled constabulary; and being mercilessly mown down. The shooting of Kelly in his unprotected legs was hardly sporting, in the circumstances.

And, most remarkable of all, the whole theatrical production was there in flesh and blood, being acted out before an audience of both friends and foes; watching, shouting, taking photographs and keeping out of harm's way. Surely there must have been a standing ovation when it was all over. It is incredible to think that at least five photographers are reported to have been at the scene, not to mention the gentlemen of the Press. The imagination warms to the men who set it up.

There are also the incidents at Jerilderie and Euroa, and the spirited night-riding, and the horse-stealing, and the making a joke of the police. Mean, sly, back-alley crime is to be feared and sneered at, but not crime conducted with such swagger and bravado. Like Mr Polly, our souls stir for the romantic, for the extravagant, vibrant, living possibilities of life amid our hum-drum, unimaginative suburban Fishbournes. We can vicariously live out our dreams in Kelly's escapades. Whilst Stringybark may shock us (though we can always rationalize it), Euroa and Jerilderie and Glenrowan hold all the bold, extravagant possibilities of the romantic life.

Again, there are Kelly's fine qualities. There is something in us which makes us forgive a man his sins so long as he is chivalrous. Moreover, Kelly rode a horse. This makes a man ten feet high, something to look up to, something quick to come and quick to go, something with that air of mystery and mastery which stirs us.

But, above all, Kelly was clad in armour. Here is the impregnable disguise for which the civilized soul yearns. One cannot help thinking of Golding's *Lord of the Flies*, of bold Jack Merridrew painting his face, disguising his features so that he could feel that neither he nor anyone else knew who he was. He acted with impunity. He killed.

He slaughtered. He savaged. He commanded. And no one could call him to account, for no one could know who he was. So perhaps with Kelly's armour.

In the imagination of all who think of Kelly stirs that faceless thing in iron, like Sidney Nolan's image of Kelly, Iron with Eyes. What reckless jaunts, what romantic exploits, what criminal escapades would we indulge in if only we could be unrecognized! Ask the soldier fighting in a foreign land. What would we not do if only we had some armour to climb into which would hide us, disguise us and protect us? All our Robin Hoods, Batmen, Supermen, Galahads ride forth in fancy dress to the Masked Ball of Romance.

Finally, let it be put bluntly, Kelly defied law and order. He stood against those processes which society had, correctly or incorrectly, set up to protect itself from itself. It could be that, like most people even in our own enlightened times, he was unable to distinguish between the processes of law and those whose job it was to uphold them. Whatever Kelly may have thought of the law of the time — or whatever we may think — it can never be forgotten that murder is murder, robbery is robbery, drunkenness is drunkenness; that the police do not fashion the law: they merely uphold it, be it good or bad.

This book is the result of the 1967 Easter Symposium on Ned Kelly set up by the Wangaratta Adult Education Centre, and held in the midst of the Kelly country. The Symposium was designed to bring academic and other informed minds to bear on what was described there as 'a shifty, dangerous, emotion-raising episode in Australian history'. It was designed to pare away the layer of myth and legend, of lies and innuendoes, of half-remembered truths and remembered half-truths, of romance and sentiment that encloses the Kelly incident; and to get at the flesh of the case, the truth of the man and his times.

Side by side with the appraisal of facts was laid existing material on Kelly: ballads, songs, plays, all of which have become part of our indigenous culture, our national heritage, an expression of our national awareness.

An exhibition of Kelly relics, documents, photographs and writings from various sources was gathered together for inspection; and a trip made through the Kelly country, where Ned, Dan, Steve Hart and Joe Byrne, their relatives, friends, and sympathizers (and the 'traps' who hunted them) rode so freely.

At the end of it all, it was difficult to decide which was the more romantic, the more exciting: the real man or the myth he has become.

This book brings together the essence of what was said, read and sung during that extraordinary weekend. It includes the talks and excerpts from the recitals; chronologies, documents, photographs and writings. It is, we believe, a fresh approach to the whole Kelly incident. It is not the end of the debate: it is in fact a perpetuation of the legend. But there is much that is new and provocative. How Ned Kelly emerges from it all is for the reader to decide.

COLIN F. CAVE

*1*

# Good Day to You, Ned Kelly

## PROFESSOR MANNING CLARK

*Professor Manning Clark was born in Sydney in 1915. He taught history at the Australian National University till 1975 and is the author of several books including the widely acclaimed* A History of Australia, *as well as short stories and articles on Australian history. He is currently working on Volume Five of his* History.

At the Hippodrome in Melbourne on 9 November 1880, four thousand people crowded inside the building and two thousand stood outside to move a resolution asking the Governor of the Colony of Victoria that the life of Edward Kelly, who had been sentenced to death for the murder of a constable, might be spared. Before the meeting began, a drunken woman created a diversion by repeating portions of the speeches which had been made by Ned Kelly during his brief life. The following morning, the Melbourne *Argus* described Kelly as one of the greatest ruffians ever to be consigned to the gallows. They went on to say that there was not a responsible citizen in the colony of Victoria of any intelligence or respectability who was not thoroughly roused against Ned Kelly. A few days later, the Sydney *Bulletin* said that society had done very little for Ned Kelly. The first recollections of his childhood, they said, were of stolen bullocks whose flesh he had helped to eat. Ned, they continued, was by nature ferocious and revengeful to the last degree, as was any man whose animal spirits had not been broken by education nor extinguished by civilization.

These pictures began to emerge after the Stringybark Creek episode in October 1878. A few months earlier Ned Kelly and Dan Kelly, with warrants out for their arrest for their part in the Fitzpatrick affair at Greta, had persuaded two of their friends, Steve Hart and Joe Byrne, to take to the Wombat Ranges. On 25 October a party of four constables, Police Sergeant Michael Kennedy, Mounted Constable Michael Scanlon, Mounted Constable Thomas Lonigan and Constable McIntyre, set out from Mansfield to hunt down Ned and Dan. To their surprise, they came upon the four of them at Stringybark Creek the following day. That same day Ned shot Kennedy, Lonigan, and Scanlon dead, and McIntyre rushed into Mansfield to give the alarm. The whole colony broke into uproar; a price was put on the head of every member of the gang. The police began their great manhunt.

On 9 December, nearly two months later, Ned and his mates raided Euroa. Again uproar, alarm and terror seized the hearts of the respectable. But this time Ned presented his case. A few days after the raid someone sent a letter addressed to a Mr Cameron, a member of the Legislative Assembly of Victoria. Ned's justification was the indignity, humiliation and pain the police had inflicted on him and his mother. Constable Lonigan had dragged him across a street in Benalla by his private parts. Constable Fitzpatrick had been guilty of 'brutal and unmanly' conduct towards his mother. As for the shooting at Stringybark Creek, those men well deserved it because they had come into the bush to shoot him down like a mad dog, even though they knew that he had been cruelly wronged. He ended with a joke. 'After all,' he added, 'so long as an outlaw reigns, the pockets of the police swell. For them 'tis double pay and country girls'. And he wound up with a good-humoured boast: 'I will oppose your laws with no offence (remember your railroads) and a sweet goodbye from

(A Forced Outlaw)!
EDWARD KELLY

Others, too, were beginning to express publicly their sympathy with Ned. In 1879 ballads in defence of Ned Kelly began to be sung in the pot-houses and tap-houses of north-eastern Victoria. Over their beer, their brandy and water, or some bushman's strong drop, and to the wail of the mouth organ, a man would sing the sardonic words:

> But brave Kelly murmured sadly as he loaded up his gun,
> O, what a bloody pity that the bugger had to run.

The respectable could detect no pity in Ned. As the *Argus* put it, the cold-blooded killing of the brave but ill-fated Kennedy was cruel, wanton and inhuman. The police, too, saw Ned as a man whose crimes had branded him with infamy. Ned, they said was a flash, ill-looking young black-guard so hardened by crime that he had become quite reckless. His brother, Dan, was a cunning, low little sneak. Steve Hart was a larrikin and a notorious horse-stealer. Joe Byrne was a fine strapping young fellow who had been corrupted into a life of crime by that prince of darkness, Ned Kelly.

At the same time at least one man urged his contemporaries to think of Ned, not with anger or loathing, but with that eye of pity recommended by the divine founder of his religion. Mindful of the command of the Galilean to have compassion on all men, and fearful lest in the coming age of unbelief men might kill each other like wild beasts, or prey on each other like the monsters of the mighty deep, Bishop Moorhouse told the people at Mansfield, to 'pity the poor wretches who have caused us to mourn over the recent disasters'. But his was a voice crying in the wilderness. The forces of law and order were already clamouring for that eye for an eye, that tooth for a tooth — for that revenge for the three brave men — Kennedy, Lonigan and Scanlon — who had lost their lives while endeavouring to capture a band of armed criminals in the Wombat Ranges near Mansfield. They were to have their satisfaction.

So, too, was Ned, doomed though he was by that madness in the blood which had caused him first to steal and then to kill. But he was to have his own moment of glory. On 8 February 1879, Ned, Dan, Joe Byrne and Steve Hart entered the town of Jerilderie, a small town in the Riverina some twenty miles inside New South Wales, bailed up the local policeman, cut off communication with the outside world, robbed a local bank, and herded the main townspeople into the Royal Mail Hotel. For days Ned lorded it over the forces he loathed and despised — the police, the bankers, and all the respectable people.

A member of the gang took a watch from the Reverend Mr Gribble, the local Methodist clergyman. With great courage Mr Gribble asked Ned to order his mate to hand the watch back. For a moment two mighty opposites confronted each other in that hotel parlour in Jerilderie. Mr Gribble represented those very forces Ned was fighting. He was that upright man who feared God and eschewed evil — that man who honoured the law and the prophets — a symbol of that giant of English philistinism, with its harsh wisdom for mankind, namely that if civilization is to prevail, then men must be like the tame geese. Ned was Irish — an outlaw, a man who had given free rein to the tempest in his blood, a man not driven on by some lofty ideal to take down the mighty from their seat, and send the rich empty away, but rather to hurt and destroy the ones who had caused the dark, undying pain to his mother, his brother, himself and men of his kind. Yet, at this moment in Jerilderie, Ned resisted the temptation to humiliate the man of law and order. He ordered his mate to hand back the watch. Mr Gribble had his moment of wisdom in that hotel parlour in Jerilderie. Sensing, perhaps, that like all the supporters of law and order, he was also a secret sharer of the unquenchable fire in Ned's heart, he bowed to him, and said, 'Good day to you, Ned Kelly'.

In the flush of success Ned dictated a second defence and justification of his actions. In this letter he moved on from the mad insensate rage of the Cameron letter to show him-

15

self and his family as victims of that ancient wrong the English had committed against the Irish:

> I have been wronged and my mother and four or five men lagged innocent and is my brothers and sisters and my mother not to be pitied also who has no alternative only to put with the brutal and cowardly conduct of a parcel of big ugly fat-necked wombat headed big bellied magpie legged narrow hipped splay-footed sons of Irish Bailiffs or English landlords.

And he went on to castigate those Irishmen like Kennedy, Lonigan, and Scanlon who

> for a lazy loafing cowardly bilit left the ash corner deserted the shamrock, the emblem of true wit and beauty to serve under a flag and nation that has destroyed massacreed and murdered their fore-fathers by the greatest of torture

Mad Ireland had fashioned Ned. His father was a Tipperary man who had been transported to Van Diemen's Land for stealing pigs. He had arrived in Hobart Town in a convict ship on 2 January 1842. Ned's mother was also Irish. She had made the long voyage as a free emigrant to Melbourne, where she had married the expiree from Van Diemen's Land, Red Kelly, and borne him a son, Edward Kelly, at Wallan in 1854. The boy probably drank in with his mother's milk that great confusion in the minds and the hearts of the Irish on questions of behaviour. The laws of God, reinforced by the harsh laws of man, forbade them to steal or to murder. God had commanded them, 'Thou shalt do no murder'. But in the pot-houses and the snugs, and out in the fields of the Emerald Isle, a man was a hero if he told one of the oppressors of his people to have his coffin ready. God had forbidden them to covet their neighbour's servant, his maid, or his ox. But again in the very air they breathed there was the assurance that to steal food from the hereditary enemies of their people was no crime.

So Ned came to man's estate a divided man — aware of the divine prohibition on theft and murder, but aware, too, that such acts against the men who had condemned 'many a blooming Irishman' to a life of tyranny were not crimes. He seems to have sensed that the English had repeated in Australia their abominations against his people — that, as he had put it in the Jerilderie letter, they had transported young Irishmen to Van Diemen's Land to pine their young lives away in starvation and misery among tyrants worse than the promised hell itself.

But on this, as on so many questions, he was wildly wrong about the historical facts of his day. He was weighed down by the dead hand of the past. Just at the time the steam engine and the railway carriage reached Wangaratta, Ned took to the horse and the saddle. Just as the drift from country to town began to gather momentum, and transport, education, and administration began to be centralized in Melbourne, Ned, in a blind fury against forces he neither understood nor felt any sympathy with, took to the Wombat Ranges. He seems to have sensed that this was a harsh country in which to earn one's daily bread. But in the deeper causes of the poverty, degradation, and misery of the selectors he took no interest. He raged against the agents of his gaolers and his oppressors — the police, and bankers — but not against the deeper reasons why he and his people had lived in such darkness, let alone showing any interest in whether mankind might one day find their way forward into the light.

He wanted to live his life, as he put it, 'fearless, free and bold', in the Greta district — and seems to have felt he could have done if it had not been for the police. He wanted to give his money to the widows and orphans and poor of Greta where he had spent many a happy day. For Ned, too, had that nostalgia for his days of innocence — as well as for that means of salvation, that yearning to be free of the guilt from his own past. But there was also that great madness in the blood, that implacable, extravagant hatred of the police — that recklessness which was driving him on to his doom. The Jerilderie Letter ends on this note of madness. He warns all those who had reason to fear him to sell out — and give ten pounds out of every hundred to the widow and orphan fund, and get out of Victoria or the consequences shall be worse than the rust in the wheat in Victoria or the druth of a dry season to the grasshoppers in New South Wales. 'I do not wish', he concludes, 'to give the order full force without giving timely warning, but I am a widow's son outlawed and my orders must be obeyed. Edward Kelly.' Ned had begun to walk into the night.

Just over a year later Ned spoke as a man who had been driven to desperation by a year in the Wombat Ranges, living with his three companions the life of the hunted and the haunted, and maddened by the loss of sympathizers as his own funds ran low, as well as by stories of the success of the police tactics of buying informers. Swept by a great gust of anger when he heard of the treachery of one Aaron Sherritt, Ned told his friends he was about to do something which would arouse the attention of the Australian colonies and of the whole world. But what that something was, he never made clear. Some said Ned had schemes for a republic of North-eastern Victoria, where, liberated from the yoke of those 'big ugly fat-necked wombat headed big bellied magpie legged narrow hipped splay-footed police men' he loathed, men could live 'fearless, free and bold'. But first he had to settle his score with Aaron Sherritt and the fat necks. Joe Byrne shot Aaron Sherritt on the night of 26 June 1880. This was to be followed by a raid on Glenrowan where the rail tracks were to be ripped up, and the train carrying the police was to hurtle downhill, killing off all the fat necks while Ned and his gang laughed at the death of men of their kind.

But it all went wrong. The rail tracks were ripped up; the people of Glenrowan were held captive in the hotel. That Sunday of 27 June the people in the hotel parlour saw both the gaiety and the madness in the men. They frolicked and danced and drank and sang the Kelly songs. But at times a great darkness swept over Ned. 'If ever I hear of you giving the police information about us,' he shouted at them, the bully in him taking over from the man with the dream of that fearless, free and bold life, 'I'll shoot you down like mad dogs.'

In the midst of that blend of gaiety, drunken laughter and terror — to the sound of merriment and squeals of delight — Curnow, the local school teacher, upright, a pillar of that respectability and tame-goose civilization Ned despised, had worked out a plan to stop the police train. He asked Ned for permission to go home. Ned let him go, saying 'Go quietly to bed, and don't dream too loud'. For the power to say the memorable thing had not deserted him at that fatal moment when his great gift for reading a man's mind in his face deserted him.

After Curnow stopped the train in the very early hours of Monday 28 June, Ned, confident as ever, boasted to the people in the hotel: 'Now you'll see some play boys. We'll shoot them all.' For, in the great crisis of his life, that daemonic hatred of the police took over so that he behaved as one possessed with an evil spirit. The dream of a fearless, free and bold life, of recapturing his days of innocence, had faded. In the early dawn Ned, wounded and dressed in his home-made armour, left the hotel possibly to contact his sympathizers, but apparently becoming faint from loss of blood he decided to return to the hotel. The police and onlookers thought for a moment as that ghostly winter dawn broke over the sombre Australian bush that it was an apparition, or an Aborigine, or a devil. Ned was walking into the world's great net. Within minutes the bullets from the fat necks had brought him down — and they had looked at him as he lay there helpless before the forces of law and order, and said, 'My God, it's Ned'.

For their will must be done. The wild man, the colonial Ishmael whose hand had been raised against every man because he believed every man's hand had been raised against him, had to be defanged if civilization was to survive. So with his three mates dead, and the hotel burning as a funeral pyre to Ned's Dionysian frenzy, Matthew Gibney, the Vicar General of the Catholic Church in Perth, who happened to be at Glenrowan, began to prepare Ned for his journey into the kingdom of perpetual night. He knew what had driven Ned mad; he knew the meaning of those words, 'Mad Ireland made him'; he knew how the English had allowed the most beautiful island on God's earth to become a land of skulls during the Great Hunger of 1846-7. But he knew too the reminder of his Divine Master that any man who was angry with his neighbour without cause was in danger of hellfire; he knew of the compassion of the Galilean for those outlaws and vagabonds who wandered over the face of the earth with a private hell in their hearts. So on that railway station at Glenrowan, Matthew Gibney began to tame Ned, and to prepare him, desperately late though it was, for redemption and acceptance — to get him to see that though men find some things right, and some wrong, to God all things are fair and just and right.

The forces of law and order then gathered for their last act with Ned. They took him to Beechworth Court, where Judge Barry had said earlier to Ned's mother those fatal words which had stirred up the madness in his blood against all policemen, judges — all those who presumed to tell him what he should do. On the way he had looked wistfully at the Strathbogie Ranges in all their majesty and wondered if he would ever see them again — for that love of the land was strong in him too. Then they took him to Melbourne, where on 28 October he was tried before a jury of twelve for 'feloniously and wilfully' murdering Mounted Constable Thomas Lonigan at Stringybark Creek two years earlier, on 26 October 1878. The following day the jury brought in their verdict of guilty. Then Mr Justice Barry, a graduate of Trinity College, Dublin, a fine flower of the Protestant ascendancy in Ireland, a violator of the Mosaic law, but not of those sections for which men hanged their kind by their necks until they were dead — a symbol of all that had provoked Ned to his impotent rage, and to his desperate quarrel with God and man, asked him whether he had anything to say. And Ned said quietly, 'I do not blame anybody,' for wisdom and grace were coming to him as the fires within him died down. And he went on to remind the learned judge that a day would come at a bigger court when they would see which was right and which was wrong.

Then Barry presented briefly the case for hanging Ned. Foolish, inconsiderate, ill-conducted, unprincipled youths unfortunately abounded, he said, who were led to imitate notorious felons, and treat men such as Ned as a hero. They must be shown the evil consequences of crime; they must be shown that a miserable death lay at the end of a life of crime. After the homily Barry solemnly pronounced the sentence of death, to which Ned added, quick as a flash, 'I will see you where I am going', for all the judges, bishops, priests, deacons, scholars, academics, lawyers and political economists — all the spiritual bullies of mankind who presume to know what was good for a man could never quite stamp out that fire.

With the *Argus* telling its readers every day that Ned was a bully, a ruffian, a coward and a larrikin, and the sympathizers and the opponents of capital punishment organizing their protest meetings, and presenting their petitions for mercy both to the government and governor of Victoria, Ned prepared to meet his fate in Melbourne jail. There on the morning of 11 November, as the Catholic priest recited the words clean different from the vision that had sustained Ned — Man that is born of woman hath but a short time to live, and is full of misery. Ned, on his last walk from the condemned cell to the place where the hangman waited, commented on the pretty flowers in the jail garden. The *Argus* writer said the jaunty air had gone and there was a frightened look in the man's eyes as he said his last words: 'Ah well, I suppose it has come to this.' Those who had loved him, as well as those who had sensed the fire of 'the

21

man within' soon replied that he had died as his mother had counselled him to — that he had died like a Kelly, saying 'Such is life.'

Outside the jail one woman went down on her knees and asked God to forgive all of them. Inside the jail, among those who had come to see the hanging, there was at least one secret sharer of that huge fire raging in Ned's heart. He was Alfred Deakin who, like Mr Gladstone in England, sensed the tempest in the blood of every man, and the final horror for those wild men who either could not or would not stop. The *Argus* on the following day reminded all criminals and larrikins that retribution for wickedness would always come at last, as it had come for Ned Kelly. A vagabond who had wandered over the face of the earth, driven on by some demon which no supporter of civilization could possibly tolerate or endure had been destroyed.

Yet Ned lived on. Despite all the sermons and homilies and leading articles, and all the attempts of the explainers, and the hounders of the weak, Ned became a folk hero. He joined Bold Jack Donahoe, Jim Jones, and that Erin's Isle hero who had suffered under Captain Logan's cruel yoke at Moreton Bay. Perhaps there is something of Australia in his story — something of that nostalgia for the life of the free, the fearless and the bold, uncorrupted by industrial civilization, with its railways, its petrol engines, and all its conformism. Perhaps there is some deeper wisdom about the meaning of life to be learned from Ned's stormy days on earth. Perhaps it is possible to see in his story, the case, as it were, for Apollo, the case for order and discipline. Perhaps we can see in it too the point about that innocent one who once walked over the face of the earth without mockery, or despair, knowing of the hell in the heart of those who said 'thou fool'. Perhaps we can recognize that the spirit of Dionysus, the frenzy that swept through Ned Kelly, lives in all of us. Like the Reverend Mr Gribble we can bow and say: 'Good day to you, Ned Kelly', and so acknowledge those gales within which, if uncontrolled, would cause us to taste deep damnation on earth as the fruit of all our disquiet.

[Following each of the individual papers, a general discussion was conducted. These discussions have been rearranged and edited for continuous reading.]

*Manning Clark:* There was no such person as Ned Kelly. Indeed, there is no such thing as a human being, in some ways. There is only what he thinks of himself at different periods of time, and what other people think of him at different periods of time. We were concerned earlier with Ned Kelly looking at himself through his own eyes and other human beings looking at Ned and his world through their eyes, at different times. It is not very likely that all people will ever look at the world in the same way — indeed, it would be terribly dull if they did!

Ned Kelly's life was very much a response to his own period. There were a number of things directly affecting his way of life. There was the coming of the railway. The arrival of the railway in Benalla and Wangaratta and the actual outbreak of the Kelly group's exploits in the district coincided in time.

As people of the time regularly pointed out, there was also obviously some connection between Kelly, his family and the landlords of Victoria. After all, a great number of the people who left the United Kingdom in the 1830s and 1840s came out here hoping to do better than they had done in the United Kingdom, and they found, in fact, that the sort of people who owned money and land in the United Kingdom also owned them in the Australian colonies. It was not going to be very much better for them. Up to a point, the Kelly outbreak was related to this enormous sense of disappointment in the migrant, both bond and free, at what happened in Australia. That is summed

23

up wonderfully in the song: *Billy Barlow,* which comes from the 1840s. In it, a man explains to his contemporaries: look, you may have thought you were going to make a fortune, but the things against you here are very much like the things which were against you in the United Kingdom.

The attitude of Ned Kelly to Australia, the land, is also worth looking at. In Sidney Nolan's paintings, for instance, you will notice that one of the many things he communicates so forcefully to us is that Ned lives on for all of us because he had some feeling for this parched, bitter continent of Australia. Kelly regularly, in speaking, saw that it was a hard, bitter country, that it was difficult for a man to drag a living out of it. Whether his violent response and the use of a gun are justifiable is a different question altogether. We must remember that once a man takes to the gun to make a response to the fact that the world has defeated him, then society must and will destroy him.

I imagine too that one of the reasons why the legend of Kelly will live on whilst there is a European-type society in Australia (and we do not know how long that will be) is that Ned Kelly addressed himself to the fundamental facts of man in this continent. He addressed himself to the suffering of the Irish, the relation between the Irish and the English. He addressed himself to the Holy Catholic Church. He addressed himself to Australia, the harsh and bitter continent. He said some interesting and memorable things. He also said that he became violent, he became savage and he had to be destroyed. I suggest to you that he lives on because he touched on things that really matter, things that concern us all.

*A. C. Clarke* [Melbourne]: For what crime was 'Red' Kelly, Ned's father, sent out?

*Manning Clark:* There are two accounts. One that he was sent out for stealing a pig: the other that he fired on a police constable.

*P. O'Hara* [Geelong]: There seems to be some doubt about the cause of the death of 'Red' Kelly. Some say he died as the result of a prison sentence he served at Kilmore: others say he just died of age and hard work. Did he actually serve the full sentence?

*Ian Jones* [A Melbourne film director and writer whose own papers appear on pages 63 and 154]: Mrs Kelly always used to say he drank brandy instead of whisky. Perhaps this had something to do with it [*laughter*]. He was out of prison when he died, and he did die of natural causes. There is no suggestion that he died as the result of harsh treatment.

*K. Hallett* [Wangaratta]: Could you please explain why Mrs Kelly was sent to jail?

*Ian Jones:* The exact charge was 'aiding and abetting in the attempted murder of a police officer'. She was tried with William Williamson and Skillion at the Spring Assizes at Beechworth, and given three years' imprisonment: Skillion and Williamson got six years' hard labour.

This does seem particularly harsh, except that this was a unique calendar. The whole district was in a demoralized condition. There were about twenty prisoners for trial at this particular Assize. Beechworth had to summon close to 140 of its total enrolment of 160 jurors. The whole business was taken particularly seriously and it was for this reason that Sir Redmond Barry (at this stage, I believe, a senior judge of the British Empire) went to Beechworth to conduct the Assize, not particularly because Mrs Kelly and her friend and son-in-law were on trial, although it is easy to place this interpretation on it. All the sentences were particularly severe. One man was given eight years for receiving a stolen horse.

It was because of this heavy calendar and the recognition of the demoralization and the need to squash the outbreak of lawlessness that these particularly hard sentences were passed.

*Judith O'Brien* [Melbourne]: It is also true, isn't it, that Mrs Kelly was arrested and tried and sent to jail with a baby in her arms?

*Ian Jones:* Yes, that is so.

*Manning Clark:* One should mention the extent of cattle

and horse-stealing in the district. The figures in the middle 1870s were astronomical. Sir Redmond Barry, who tried Mrs Kelly, is reported to have said: 'If your son were here, I'd give him an even harder sentence.' Ned knew this later on when he found Judge Barry trying him on a capital charge in Melbourne. This may help to explain the liveliness of the exchange between Barry and Kelly on that occasion.

*Ian Jones:* I am interested in this story about Sir Redmond Barry. It is often quoted, but I would like to be able to find an authority. Although Mrs Kelly's case was fully reported by a number of papers, none of them mentioned Barry's remark. It would have made wonderful copy.

*Question* [from the floor]: Somewhere I have heard that the mother, who must also have had a great influence on the children, was a very hardy, tough woman. Was there not an incident where she broke a spade over a policeman's head?

*Ian Jones:* That was poor old Fitzpatrick.

*Mrs M. Kirkwood* [Benalla]: I would like to refer, if I may, to the Fitzpatrick episode, when Constable Fitzpatrick went to the Greta home after the Kellys. This was to enforce the law and order which Professor Clark said 'must be obeyed'.

Victoria was then a new colony and the law was very young, very new. Again, many people who came out found these laws to be very like the ones they had tried to escape from in the United Kingdom. For Kelly, too, the laws were not *just* laws. I do not mean the law that applied after his capture, but the laws that applied to the selectors and the squatters etc. That gave rise to all the unrest, and caused the police official — Nicholson, I think his name was — to say that no police constable must go to the Kelly homestead on his own and also that the Kellys and their ilk were to be picked up on any paltry charges and sent to Pentridge, to stamp out this unrest. Constable Fitzpatrick went to the Kelly homestead against these orders. He took a considerable time to get there, stopping at the pub on the way. Did he intended to apprehend Dan Kelly and take him single-handed from the home of the Kellys?

If we are going to blame Kelly for the Fitzpatrick episode, we must remember that we have only Fitzpatrick's word for what went on, and he was later dismissed from the police force as 'a liar and a larrakin'.

*Hon T. Mitchell* [Corryong]: Mrs Kirkwood spoke of Victoria being a new colony with a new law. That might be so; but Victoria at that stage had had only twenty years of separate political entity. At the same time, this whole area had been part of New South Wales for some seventy years. Therefore for nearly a hundred years there had been a system of law over this particular area. I find it a bit hard to see, then, that the Kellys were faced with 'a new law' in 'a new colony'.

*Manning Clark:* The whole question of the police is related to things which probably touched Ned Kelly deeply in his own life.

Ned's father came from Tipperary with a background of distrust of the Anglo-Saxon which certainly influenced his children. He arrived in Van Diemen's Land in 1842, five years after the departure of Colonel Arthur from Tasmania.

Now, Colonel Arthur was a very high-minded man, a very noble man, but, for a variety of reasons which need not concern us now, he was increasingly forced to use convicts and ex-convicts as policemen. There was a great agitation against this procedure in Tasmania, commonly known as the agitation against the Felon Police. 'Red' Kelly must have been very confused by all this talk against the felon police, and against the English, the great anger about the use of felon police to arrest and pry into the affairs of the so-called 'free men'. Kelly was not the only Vandemonian to come across to Victoria with this background.

When Edward Kelly faced up to the police, they were not felon police, not convict police; what is more, they were partly Irish themselves. Here Kelly is shooting at Irishmen. This was all very paradoxical.

There is no simple, straight explanation for Kelly's attitude to the police but it would probably have to be traced right back to his father who must have influenced his children about the police in Australia from a Tasmanian background rather than a Victorian or New South Wales one.

*Weston Bate* [A senior lecturer in Australian History at Melbourne University and the author of the paper on page 40]: Naturally, the business of understanding how Ned was influenced is conjecture. What one does get in the police files (and I have particularly examined the Benalla police of 1870) is the constant mention of the Quinn family. There is quite a contrast between the picture of the Quinn family given to us by Max Brown in *Australian Son*[1] and the picture revealed by the police files.

The event which set me puzzling most occurred at Greta. It raises the question again of how one deals with the Kellys and the Quinns.

There is a graphic description of a chase by Constable Hall, in charge at Greta with an assistant named, curiously enough, Archdeacon. Hall relates, in a memo to Benalla, that James and Pat Quinn came chasing young Ned Kelly (this was in 1870, when Kelly was sixteen) and Ned took refuge by throwing himself off his horse on to the veranda of the Greta Police Station. It was then that, according to Hall, he arrested Quinn by pulling him off his horse, but, while he was doing this, Pat Quinn hit him with a stirrup iron and Hall had an injury to show for this. We are not sure how serious this injury was. How much *do* the police report things their own way, especially in this case when they are so worried about this group of men 'beneath the law'?

This quaint business of Ned Kelly running away from his uncles has fascinated me and made me wonder just what was the role of the police at that time. I would like to say that I think Mrs Kirkwood's point about Fitzpatrick and

---

[1] Max Brown, *Australian Son; The Story of Ned Kelly* (Georgian House, Melbourne 2nd. ed., 1956). A biography, which includes the Jerilderie Letter.

the fact that Fitzpatrick's testimony was the one Judge Barry was interested in at Beechworth indicates a general concern with law and order and the long history of Mrs Kelly and the Quinn family. Ned was getting it with both barrels.

*Manning Clark:* Mrs Kelly must have been an enormous influence on Ned Kelly. But she is a blank page; we know very little about her. Once again, we are depending upon whose eyes we are looking through — those of the Chairman of the Royal Commission, or of many people who gave evidence there, arraying themselves time and time again on the side of law and order, saying that it was absurd to say that Kelly was persecuted. But, if we look at Ned speaking, this is the main point he makes. He claims that he, his mother, and all his family were persecuted. Who is right? Either we accept one pair of eyes or the other, or assume a state of tremendous arrogance and become one of God's spies, looking down on the whole thing.

*Ian Jones:* On this question of Ned Kelly's attitude to law, the machinery of justice, responsibility to the community and so on, it is easy to believe that Kelly was a complete rebel. But there is a deal of evidence against this.

After his first serious prison term, Ned Kelly did lead an effective and honest life. There are three years in which he was a person of some substance, quite looked up to.

Perhaps it is not generally recognized that Constable Fitzpatrick was, at one stage, a friend of the Kelly family, quite a close friend. Now, the incident at Benalla when Ned got drunk spectacularly ended this friendship.

Ned, you remember, was drunk (how he got drunk is the question?), rode his horse across the footpath, was arrested by a group of police and taken to the lockup. The following morning, Fitzpatrick was most anxious that his 'mate' Ned Kelly should be handcuffed on the way to the courthouse. This surely is suspicious behaviour.

It was also the only time that anyone ever saw Ned Kelly drunk. I would be delighted if anyone has any other information on that point. He is on record as drinking some prodigious quantities of liquor, before and after his capture at Glenrowan, but at no stage was he deemed to be drunk.

On this one occasion in Benalla, however, he did get drunk. It does tend to look as though Fitzpatrick, who had not been showing up terribly well as a constable and who had been kicking up his heels and hob-nobbing with the Kellys, had decided upon a spectacular *coup* to regain his reputation. Eventually Kelly broke away from the police and there followed the brawl with two troopers and the bootmaker in the old bootmaker's shop, after which Ned Kelly let himself be led away by old Mr McInnis, the Justice of the Peace. He happily went to the court-house and was happily fined £2.10.0 for damage to police uniforms, drunkenness and one or two other things.

It was only a matter of weeks after this that Dan Kelly and Tom Lloyd were in trouble over a rather confused prank at a store in which there had been some degree of assault on a woman. Both boys took to the bush. Fitzpatrick gave evidence before the Royal Commission that he saw Ned Kelly some little time after this. Ned Kelly had already been approached by an Inspector to persuade Dan Kelly and Tom Lloyd to surrender. It was Fitzpatrick who persuaded Ned Kelly to arrange the surrender of the two. Ned Kelly led them into Benalla; they stood for trial and both received quite heavy sentences on what, it is alleged, was perjured evidence, and Tom Lloyd was subsequently given an additional sentence for rape.

Ned Kelly, as far as British justice and its machinery was concerned, was 'twice bitten and three times shy'.

*F. Gardner* [Melbourne]: Professor, you raised the question: who was Ned Kelly? What of the far deeper question: was Ned Kelly good or bad? In his progress, uncharted and unguided, he did things to give him some magnitude as an able and outstanding man. He had the range of human feelings, as you have pointed out, he was magnanimous and so on, and in that sense you granted he was a good man.

But, he came up against the blank wall of law and order

and had to be destroyed, you say. We must say that, certainly at that stage, the law was not very good. Was not there some good in the relation of Kelly to injustice and inequality?

*Manning Clark:* I am glad you raised that point. When I said: 'He must be destroyed', I did not mean to imply that I am a believer in capital punishment. I am not. I did not mean to imply, although it may have sounded like that, that Ned *had to be hanged.* One of the interesting things about this case is that the opposition to his execution did not come just from the criminal classes or the larrikins or the deluded or those who had nothing to do.

There was a serious movement against capital punishment at the end of the 1870s. There were some terrible hangings in Hobart early in the nineteenth century. And a Mr Taylor of Hobart, in that environment, had bravely come forward as an advocate for the abolition of capital punishment. He and those who strongly believed in him (and there were many) were behind the demonstrations against the hanging of Ned Kelly. Mr Gaunson, who took the chair at public meetings and was also Chairman of Committees in the Victorian Parliament, took the chair not because he agreed with the lawlessness of Ned Kelly but because he was not happy about the use of capital punishment. It is impossible to tell how many people were advocating the reprieve of Ned Kelly simply because they were against capital punishment. Mr Gaunson seemed to be arguing that Kelly was dangerous, but he should not be hanged. But, in that sense, law and order must protect society against people like Kelly, who were going to shoot other people. It does not necessarily follow that society has to *hang* them.

At that point we could have a serious discussion around Kelly, because he was a focal point — not just about England *v.* Ireland, or Man *v.* Environment, in Australia, but about capital punishment itself.

I notice that the Press of the time announced that the politicians Sir Henry Parkes of New South Wales, and Sir

John Robertson of New South Wales, were both against capital punishment. It would seem at the time that Victorians were much stronger advocates of capital punishment than were the people of New South Wales and Tasmania.

*Question* [from the floor]: Was there not a great danger at this time of the Kellys influencing the younger people, to whom he was something of a God, if the action had not been taken? Would not there have been the danger of young people following Kelly's suit, particularly as Kelly's boasting was 'making a mockery of the law'?

*Manning Clark:* It was certainly true that some of those who wanted to deal with Ned Kelly felt there had to be a public example, and the only effective example was capital punishment. It is up to you to decide whether they were right or wrong.

Kelly not only appealed to the criminals and the larrikins. He was a hero to a large number of people in the Australian colonies. These people had to be shown that this was a delusion, that such behaviour requires retribution. This argument was repeated, be it right or wrong, time and time again.

All kinds of people come into this argument. For instance, the Chairman of the Royal Commission which was held later, was Francis Longmore, a member of the Victorian Parliament. If you look at that Commission, you will notice that from time to time, the Chairman was anxious to find out: was Ned drunk? Was Dan drunk? Was Steve Hart drunk? Was Joe Byrne drunk? I consulted comments by another very upright man, Mr Alfred Deakin, to see what he thought of Longmore and learned two things:

(1) Longmore was the Chairman of the Temperance Movement in Victoria. He naturally wanted to know how much strong drink the gang was putting away during the campaign.

(2) Deakin says that Longmore was a very harsh judge. Much of the excellent summary of the Royal Commission

(the harsh parts possibly, I imagine), comes from this rather harsh Chairman. These judgments about Ned are the ones which are repeated most often. The word 'ruffian' comes from the Melbourne *Argus,* but was repeated by Longmore. That was the way he saw the world.

One is brought back to the problem: what was the truth about Ned? Mr Longmore's Royal Commission is the truth as seen through the eyes of a harsh temperance man.

*Miss J. Dunn* [Monash University]: What was the attitude of the people of the Kelly country? Were they in favour of this capital punishment or would they rather have seen him serve a prison sentence?

*Manning Clark:* In evidence before the Royal Commission a number of the people of the local area said that it was difficult to tell how many sympathizers there were, who was liked, who was disliked, and so on, because, as it moved on, law and order bred terror.

If we take Curnow as a very honest and truthful man, a very courageous man, his testimony is worth looking at. He says time and time again that, on Kelly matters, people were not game to talk to each other. On Kelly matters in this district, he only trusted his wife. Other people said similar things.

This is an interesting phenomenon in society (we don't know it very often in our country) —a situation where people have to be worried about what they say. I have seen it in different sorts of society — in Germany before the war, and, possibly in one other society, where people are worried about what they say. There is some element of this in the South in America amongst the Negroes. It takes an enormous amount of courage to say things publicly when you know that whatever you say may rebound against you.

So when people say that there were hundreds or thousands of sympathizers for Kelly, you need to say: how do you know for certain? Has anyone ever told the truth on this subject, when people are afraid to speak about it?

*Hon T. Mitchell* [Corryong]: I would like to throw in something my late father told me in 1916, that the success of Kelly's attack on Jerilderie was due to the strategy of Ned Kelly himself. Ned made a boast that no New South Wales policeman would ever stop him getting into New South Wales and that he was going to attack Jerilderie.

As a result of this boast, the New South Wales police lined the New South Wales border and waited for Kelly. Kelly and his gang, having brought that about, then proceeded to go right round through the north-east, crossed the river at Upper Towong, went right round behind the line of waiting New South Wales constables, and held Jerilderie in their power very successfully for a week.

*Dewar Goode* [Melbourne]: Whilst there is great historic interest in Ned Kelly as a bushranger, I feel that we should also take into account that he was a good bushman. He was bad in most other things but, as a bushman and a man who lived off the land, he must have been exceptional. I wonder if there has been much research into this particular aspect of the man?

*Ian Jones:* Constable McIntyre, who could hardly be considered a public relations man for the Kelly gang, said in his account of Stringybark Creek some time after the event, that the Kelly gang were the best shots, the best bushmen and the best horsemen the colony could produce. This seems to be accurate. We know only a little about Ned's bushcraft, but we can assume from the way the gang moved at night through incredibly rough country that they were great bushmen.

After Stringybark Creek, when they were heading north across the Murray, they were riding four horses and driving six, and yet they managed to average about forty to fifty miles a day, through flooded creeks and much swampy country. This was quite a feat.

Superintendent Hare, in his evidence before the Royal Commission, mentions a night in the Ranges near Beechworth on which the running water was freezing in the creeks, when some of the troopers who were quite capable bushmen were wrapped up in possum-skin rugs trying to keep warm, he found Sherritt curled up on the ground in his shirt-sleeves. McIntyre was a little shaken by this and, next morning, asked Aaron whether the Kellys were as tough as he. Sherritt replied: 'I'm tougher than Joe, and I can lick the two youngsters. But Ned's tougher than I am. I regard him as superhuman.'

This is surely the most spectacular comment you could make on Kelly's toughness as a bushman.

*Question:* At Glenrowan, why was it necessary for Curnow to stop the train where he did when, within a few more hundred yards, it would have reached the Glenrowan platform?

*Hon T. Mitchell* [Corryong]: This is a very interesting question. Why did Curnow go out to stop the train south of Glenrowan? First: the quicker you get information to your friends in an emergency the better. Second: where was the train going? If it was sent for urgently and was going through to Beechworth after the murder of Aaron Sherritt, the train was probably not going to stop at Glenrowan anyway. Third: if the train was going to stop at Glenrowan would anyone, in view of the proximity of Mrs Jones's 'pub', walk up knowing that the trigger-happy Kellys were waiting just behind them? Curnow, as has been implied, was going down the line expecting to get a bullet in his back at any moment. Finally, where exactly was the track pulled up in relation to the station? Quite obviously the Kellys expected it to go through and the broken rails must have been fairly close, within walking distance. Obviously then, Curnow needed to go *down* the line to stop the train effectively.

*N. McKissock* [Bright]: On the north side, the rail goes downhill. About half a mile beyond the Glenrowan station, on the right of the rail, is a gorge. It was at approximately this point that the Kellys ordered the fettlers to break the rail and direct them down the gorge. They gambled on the police going right through, thinking that the Kelly gang was around the Beechworth area. Had the train continued, the police would have been lost in the gorge and the Kellys would have had Benalla at their mercy.

*K. Embling* [Glenrowan]: I have not lived in Glenrowan all my life, just since the last war, but I know the area and its people well. Ned Kelly was an Irish larrikin who lost his father at eleven years of age. He had a strong-willed mother, and many brothers and sisters. Ned, at a very tender age, was left to provide for this family of 'wild Irishmen'. He stole. He did what any young fellow would do. He took what was necessary, a chook here, a pig there; and he was warned by the police. What was he to do to keep his family alive?

When they left Digger's Rest and came to Glenrowan, the family settled down to lead a more or less normal life. Let us project ourselves back into the 1870s, when life was not as we know it. That country then was very wild indeed. The Kellys were trying to wrest a living out of the bush. They were wild, we know they were wild. They were people who idealized wild riding, wild times, going into Greta, racing up and down and having a good time in the pub. What else could the young blade in those days do when he lived in the country?

But, have we been told that Ned was also a leader? He was a saw mill manager for a time. He led an honest life for some years, until he was hounded, and I agree with Mrs Kirkwood that he *was* hounded. The incident of Fitzpatrick with his mother, rather than his childhood misdemeanours as a provider for his family, turned him against law and order. He idolized his mother. When she was put into jail he considered this the grossest injustice of all. What was he to do? He went, a poor man, to look for money to pay a lawyer. He stole that money. A great deal of the money went to pay his lawyer to try to keep his mother from jail. He did not use it for himself. He wanted to have his mother released from what he considered was an injustice.

Ned was a larrikin like a lot of other young fellows of those days, and he could not keep his eyes off a good horse. Locally, there is the story that when he was being chased by the police, about half-way between Glenrowan and

Winton, he came to one of the blacksmith's shops which, in those days, were spaced every five to seven miles. Ned himself was a most proficient blacksmith. Knowing the police were close, with blacktrackers, he himself re-shoed his horse in reverse to deceive the police. It takes a good blacksmith to do that. This illustrates his horsemanship and skill, if nothing else.

Why has he become a legend? He was hounded, he was taught as a boy to steal because he had to. He idolized his mother. He was a leader of men. He was a fine bushman. And through all he was brought (was it?) to justice.

*Hon T. Mitchell:* An important point has been touched on. The Kelly gang enjoys its prominence for two reasons.

First: the Kellys were the last of the bushrangers. Had there been other gangs afterwards, I doubt if we would have remembered the Kellys with the interest and clarity we do today. They were the end of an era.

Second: the Kellys had to face a certain set of circumstances that the original bushrangers, Morgan, Starlight, Moonlight, Gilbert, Power, O'Malley and Hall, and all those others did not have to face. The Kellys had to face a much better police force. Undoubtedly, the type of man employed as policemen in New South Wales and Victoria in the earliest days was not nearly as good as the type of man in the force at the time the Kellys came on the scene. Again, they had to deal with much better mounted police. In the old days the police had any old nag that the Department would dish out to them; the bushrangers had the pick of the squatters' race-horses. The police had as little chance of catching the bushrangers as the police had, in later days, of catching the fast transports on the Hume Highway. Finally, they had to deal with quick means of communication — the railways and the telegraph.

It was largely because they had to combat difficulties (and for many years they overcame them) which the early bushrangers did not have to deal with that the Kellys have assumed this position of prominence in the fabric of our Australian history.

*Manning Clark:* I find it most fascinating to hear people talk about what this is all about because, I take it, it helps us all to advance our knowledge of the country in which we live. There are moments in the history of the country in which an event forces people to think about our history and our destiny. Certainly this man Ned Kelly had something which encouraged people to think about fundamental things in our history; much as they were forced to do by the events of 1914 and in 1941. I am not suggesting for a moment that Kelly was a man to match the happenings of 1914 and 1941, but he did raise the whole question of law and order in a civilized society.

I agree with Mrs Kirkwood that it is quite likely that Constable Fitzpatrick behaved in a way which provoked, even maddened, Kelly, but that is an act of chance. If Fitzpatrick had not done it, I imagine someone else would have. It seems quite likely that the police did lose their heads for a while. After all, they were confronted with a great problem. There was an outbreak of disorder, of anarchy, and it was their function to restore order. It is perfectly true, as I see it, that there were a number of people who did not accept these laws. They felt that they contradicted natural and divine law, and, in as far as they did this, these people felt that they did not owe obedience to the laws.

Kelly raised this whole question of what a man deserves to get. He certainly believed that a great injustice had been perpetrated against his whole family and he came later to feel that a great injustice had also happened to the people. But, of course, there were a great number of contradictions. After all's said and done, we have talked about him as Irish and Catholic. But, when Mrs Kelly married for the second time, she was married by a Methodist clergyman. We talked about Ned getting angry with the Anglo-Saxon, but he was shooting at Kennedy, Lonigan and Scanlon, all Irishmen.

We ought to realize that Ned Kelly was confronted by a situation which was too big for him. He was brought down;

he had to be brought down. I feel, and I may be quite wrong, that he eventually saw this; he saw that there was something much bigger in all this. He came to accept it very late in his life.

I imagine that he is going to live on because he touched on things that really matter.

## 2

# Kelly and His Times

WESTON BATE

*Weston Bate is in his mid-fifties and has been Professor of Australian Studies at Deakin University since 1978. At the time this paper was delivered he was Senior Lecturer in charge of Australian History, Melbourne University. He is the author of* A History of Brighton *(1952) and* Lucky City *(1978), the first volume of a history of Ballarat.*

This is a large topic, for it involves *the truth* about Ned. But that's what we have come for, though I must admit I am a trifle disconcerted that Professor Clark suggests that three truths are encapsulated in any one truth it is possible to lay down — the truth according to the sympathizers, the opponents and the explainers, to which last group I know I am professionally attached.

I will not attempt to find a total explanation of any event, nor an explanation of the total event. But I will try to set out what needs to be explained. First we must account for Ned Kelly himself. How did he become the kind of man he was? Secondly, we need to discover the reasons for the support he had, and then the reasons for the failure of the police to deal with him more quickly than they did. Finally, I believe we must try to explain the rapid growth of the Kelly legend.

There is an underlying explanation of Ned Kelly in the economics of the period, the best outline of which has been given by N. G. Butlin, in his *Investment in Economic*

*Development in Australia 1860-1900.* And I would like to suggest that you note carefully Butlin's view that urban development was a dominant feature of the period in Australia, and that manufacturing was the fastest growing area of the economy. Land settlement was important, but it was not decisive. It is especially important to notice the tendency to centralize business and administration in the capital city of each state. Urban residents controlled the development of the states. They used large amounts of capital for urban building and the capital put into railway building was used to create a radial network that led trade in Victoria, for instance, back into the pockets of the Melbourne merchants and financiers.

The railways were tremendously important in the transformation from a grazing country to a farming one. In the north-east [of Victoria] the railway reached Wangaratta in October 1873, and immediately it had a great effect. Indeed, it had various effects, but one of them in particular is indicated in the local paper in 1877. At Albury, during harvest, the strippers — a term it is dangerous to use nowadays — were 'hard at it,' although there were complaints of a scarcity of strippers because of a combination of operators. They were banking on the inability of farmers to hold their grain, though what the paper noticed was that the railways had made it better for people who were close to the line. They could rely on regular transport and did not have to supply their own storage facilities, or depend upon the weather keeping roads open at the right time. Farms improved rapidly. Witness an advertisement in 1877 for a farm of 212 acres on the Ovens flats where the soil was 'exceedingly rich, adapted for cereals, tobacco and hops'. The property was substantially enclosed and divided into six paddocks. Ninety acres were cleared and forty acres sown down with English grass and clover. It sold at £5.15.0 an acre. This of course isn't just the railways, but it is a sign of the maturity of farming in certain areas of the north-east. If the land was fertile, and they had the capital to get going, there was a very profitable future for those who had

41

been lucky enough to get it. But, and this is the big *but,* it was those who had capital who were to benefit, or who had acquired farming skills in areas nearer the coast in earlier periods. People like the Kellys weren't to be included in their ranks. Thus, although the transformation of the north-east was quite rapid, many people missed out.

Now I want to talk about centralization as an explanation of the Kelly outbreak. Centralized administration was a feature of the police force according to the Royal Commission of 1882. The local police were not always as well served as the metropolitan and one of the very interesting things about the Royal Commission (and this goes with Professor Clark's point about the chairman's interest as a teetotaller), is the time taken in questioning police in the metropolitan area about their dealings with prostitutes and after-hours traders and their general behaviour towards public houses. There was a great deal of recrimination between the city magistrates and the police in this Royal Commission, and there seems to be quite a different atmosphere in the metropolis, and in the higher ranks of the police force, than there is in the outer areas. And, as far as I can tell, there is not a great conception of how you deal with people like Edward Kelly, his brother and friends.

The lands administration was also highly centralized. Every action over a selector was reported to Melbourne for comment. And I have noticed from the documents that there was a very important gap between the locality and the centre. In many cases squatters and large landowners received more sympathetic treatment than the small man who could not put his point well. Rich men had friends or agents in Melbourne who could handle any problem with the lands administration.

The third major aspect was the centralization of politics. I agree with Mrs Kirkwood's remark that it is important to stress the rawness of the colony and the inexperience of its legislators. But the laws were basically English law, and they followed an English pattern Ned Kelly was bound to argue against. They supported the cause of the propertied man against the man of little property, and they were certainly based on attitudes of Anglo-Saxon superiority. They were the laws of the middle class. The Victorian parliament, which was inclined to pride itself on being a democratic parliament, was very much held back in its approach to democracy by the position of an intransigent upper house where the propertied interest was dominant. From 1877 to 1880, in a Premiership that gained the support of the Melbourne mob and many thinking men like Alfred Deakin, Graham Berry endeavoured to break the stranglehold of the Legislative Council and in doing so stirred up much class bitterness. But this was mainly on the surface. Basically the community was united in its pursuit of material gain, and politicians unblushingly bargained and bartered their votes in the house for benefits in their electorates. The centralization of politics meant that any member from distant parts could find himself very important to the government on particular moves and his support could be bought for a local railway or for any local benefits that were important to him. So you get electoral speeches like that of a famous member for the Moira constituency in the Lower House, Mr P. Hanna, who regretted that the railway bills of 1877 had not been made law. He wanted all sorts of railways through his electorate; from Avenell to Shepparton, from Waurn Springs to Wahgunyah, which he believed had been stonewalled by obstructionists and office seekers. The north-east railway having been a success he hoped to see provision made in the next railway bill for lines from Benalla to Yarrawonga, Shepparton to Dookie, Wangaratta to Oxley and Moyhu, and Benalla to Mansfield. All of these brought him votes. The point of the illustration is that government depended very much upon logrolling.

But the railway was to be, more than anything, as has already been suggested, a fillip to Melbourne business interests who had little time to consider the deeper needs of distant localities. The same goes for the centralizing tendency of the head offices of the banks in Melbourne. They

43

determined bank policy and gave their orders to the managers in distant parts without much regard for the needs of local residents. And here we should note the hatred and suspicion that Kelly showed not only in particular against the Bank of New South Wales, but against all banks in his area.

There was similar feeling about the provision of courts of justice. Beechworth did not have courts when it was convenient to the locality, but when it was convenient to judges from Melbourne. Often there would be a criminal court one month, and not again for six. Criminals would have to be kept in jail waiting for these courts to sit.

Before leaving the question of centralization I would like to highlight the condition of the police, and to suggest that the centralized accounts system was a hindrance to mobility and initiative in local areas, because the communication of ideas and the communication of experience was extremely limited in the police force. A constable who incurred any expense while on duty had to put in a complicated series of requisitions, all of which tended to clog up the work of the police. Long memos exist throughout police records about the cost of stabling this or that horse, and whether it ought to be a charge on departmental funds. There was also a tendency for the men in Melbourne to be howlers of calamity when trouble arose at a distance. In August 1870, for instance, Chief Commissioner Standish wrote the following memo about James Quinn, Ned Kelly's uncle: 'I hope every exertion will be made to apprehend Quinn. He is not unlikely to take to the bush, and will be a far more dangerous criminal than Power ever was.' Quinn gave himself up the same day, and his brother Pat was also brought in without resistance.

A question to which I think we might address ourselves in the general context of the police and the way they treated people is this dissociation between locality and centre. Did those at the centre know what was happening? And, more important, weren't they trying to create an impression of disturbed law and order so that administratively they could sound the alarm that would put them on a much more, shall we say, emotionally effective basis for their kind of police work?

Mind you, the local police were clearly confused about the seriousness of the Greta mob as a threat to law and order. Superintendent Nicholas of Benalla, who was in charge of the whole north-east, made various conflicting statements. In August 1870, he said, 'Greta is now quiet and can be reduced to one constable. There is insufficient work for two mounted men, I only recommended two while Power was at large, and having numerous local associates, the Quinns and the Kellys.' But on 17 November 'Young Kelly was a terror to the locality, and persons were afraid to prosecute him.' He thought it very probable, as stated by Hall, the constable at Greta, that Kelly would join Lowry, a bushranger of the time, and go into the bush. Yet in the same period Kelly took refuge with Constable Hall when fleeing from his two uncles. All I can suggest is that the views of the police are puzzling. What were they emphasizing? How significant was the area of lawlessness around Greta when the Quinns gave themselves up, and when young Kelly threw himself at the mercy of a policeman? I am suspicious of Constable Hall's account of what happened when the Quinn brothers wounded him. Certainly a clearer understanding of the nature of his wound and how it came about would be a help, because it is pretty hard to see why these desperate men, who were going to take Hall's life (so he said) with their stirrup irons, gave themselves up so easily. And we have heard other evidence of these men handing themselves over to the police — or of Kelly helping to hand them over, or whatever went on.

This is an appropriate point at which to leave the theme of centralization and discuss the role of class antagonism in the Kelly outbreak. Class antagonism has been well documented in this period, and you will find interesting accounts of it in Russel Ward's *Australian Legend,* in Furphy's *Such is Life* and Brown's *Australian Son,* as well as in Charles Dilke, and many others who observed Vic-

torian society at this time. Victorian society was not democratic, and clearly within the district the sources of class
antagonism were economic (predominance of the squatter
and large land holder) and traditional. The latter antagonisms are those that Professor Clark talked so clearly about
— national and religious. All of them were strongly held by
the men of Greta.

On whose terms was life being lived in this area? Here
we return to whether one believes Mrs Kelly, a mighty
wielder of the shovel apparently, or Constable Fitzpatrick,
who, according to the Royal Commission, was not a man to
be relied upon. I will be very interested in the views of
Mr Jones and Professor Waller about how much the liar
Fitzpatrick's evidence was important in the condemnation
of Mrs Kelly and the very heavy sentence of three years
which she received in 1878.

There are many signs of distrust of the upper class
throughout the period in this area and class antagonisms are
shown in attitudes to property. They come out perhaps
most in sheep-stealing. Squatter McBean of Kilfera station
had some sheep taken. He called the police, and they
tracked down some of his station hands who had sheep
skins at their hut. There was no evidence that these were
McBean's sheep skins, but naturally station hands should
not have sheep skins, and must be considered the sheep-
stealers. Now this is fair enough, I suppose, because property must be protected and the squatter doesn't want to
lose any sheep. But the interesting aspect of the case was the
leniency of a Benalla magistrate who, instead of committing
the men for trial for sheep stealing, fined them very lightly
indeed. The editor of the local paper protested that this
was the most flagrant case of dereliction of duty that had
ever occurred in the Australian colonies — a crime which
meant death in the old country, or severe imprisonment
in this one, had been condoned. He was clearly not concerned about the shakiness of the evidence. And there was
a letter from 'Fair Play' (such people always sign themselves 'Fair Play') complaining about the lenient sentence.

Until now he said, we have had sentences of three to seven years for sheep stealing. Finally there was a letter from Mr McBean himself who warms one's heart even though one feels that he might not always have treated the law, especially the land law, with respect. He had a sense of humour. In large letters he had printed in the paper;

TO SHEEP STEALERS, IN CONSEQUENCE OF THE DECISION OF THE MAGISTRATE IN THE BENALLA COURT, THE UNDERSIGNED WILL BE OBLIGED IF SHEEP STEALERS WILL TAKE ONLY WHAT MUTTON THEY REQUIRE FOR PRIVATE USE.

On whose terms was life being lived? Selection had been an attempt to help. It wasn't just centralized bureaucracy; it was the government at the centre acting under democratic pressures, in a way that it believed would assist the development of the country. But it was also prompted by an ideal that you could change men by settling them on the land. Clive Turnbull, in his excellent *Concise History of Australia,* has printed an eloquent cartoon from an English paper of the time which shows on the one hand a family group in an English slum — father, mother, and three or four children in rags. Behind them, alongside each other, are advertisements for Chartist meetings and government notices banning them. This is evidence of social unrest of a very important kind. But on the other side of the picture we see the same family in the antipodes. Father, mother and children are gathered around the festive board of a quite respectable dwelling. Father is carving a big leg of mutton with obvious relish, while one of the girls hands a meal out the window to an aborigine. The picture expresses the idealism of the upper classes of this period. They saw colonial land settlement as a safety valve, a method of dealing with the lower classes in England, and a return to the golden age of the sturdy yeoman. Sure, you pick 'em up, take 'em out there, and hey presto they're fine fellows . . . Like Ned Kelly? The myth of how easily this could be done

47

is the great myth of Australian settlement. From the days of Edward Gibbon Wakefield onwards, people were to suffer for this, because the motivation (fear of the lower classes) was transmitted to the colony. In many ways it was fear, not idealism, that led politicans to pass the Selection Acts. Mind you, the arguments they used about the virtues of life on the land were accepted by people who wanted to improve their position, but who had no capital. They believed in the genuineness of the government's attempt, and in their right to have land. What happened we all know. On the whole, men with money and who could command credit, succeeded, or men with farming experience who were prepared to work very hard. It was nothing like as easy as had been suggested.

In such circumstances it is not surprising that, like the Kellys, some took the easier way of dealing in the stock of people who were doing well. They had felt the injustice of the way the squatter could muster his team of dummies and tie up the best land in the whole district. And they argued quite directly that if these men could do what they wanted with the law by taking land far beyond their rights, why should sheep-stealing or horse-stealing be such a desperate crime? This, I think, is the relative morality of the period. One can't say that the Kellys were honest, but one can say that they must be seen against the general disregard of ethics and morality by people of all classes intent on making money. During the land boom (later in Victorian history) morality meant nothing to men with money, as you can find out from Michael Cannon's book *The Land Boomers*. Not only were their actions condoned but their guilt was hushed up by clever use of the law. Is it any wonder that Kelly's Jerilderie letter contained much evidence of class antagonism? Kelly based his picture of society on the wrong done to the small man. There seemed to be one law for the rich, like Whitty and Burns, and one law for the poor in this lovely country.

Horse-stealing seems to have been the worst crime of all, because a horse was the most prized possession of the men of this period. Horse racing had become a national institution even then, and its roots extended very firmly right through society. With a horse, as you know from Ned Kelly's escapades, a man became free. And a man who was as eloquent on a horse as was Ned Kelly became dramatically free. His horse was a symbol to him of his freedom from the difficult path of trying to be a bona fide selector under conditions in which most bona fide selectors without capital were trampled on. The people without capital who became established as bona fide selectors were mainly, as far as I can tell, those who selected under the 42nd clause of the 1865 Act, who were within a reasonable range of the gold fields, and who could mine part-time, or had other part-time sources of income at hand, and who were lucky enough to select ground that could reasonably quickly be made payable.

Now I think it important to turn in an explanatory way to the philosophical basis for the revolt. Here I am bold enough to disagree again with the local member, for it seems to me that the Kelly affair was not an affair of bushrangers but of outlaws. It had quite a different context from the usual bushranger picture. I am not an authority about this, but it seems to me that in this area there was a mass of dead end lives, which may explain the Kelly legend. Men who had little hope were sympathetic to, and might well take, Ned Kelly's road to the freedom of the bush and to the defiance of a law which they had grounds to feel had been a rotten law. The degraded conditions of the slums of the metropolis, which occupied social thinkers a great deal, were nothing to the degraded conditions of people living in these rural areas. Think of it in terms of human dignity. A widow in a bark hut right here in Wangaratta in the 1870s was the chief witness in a case of attempted rape. She described the circumstances. A man came to her door, which was a slab of bark and, as he couldn't move it at first, he was deferential enough to feel around the walls for some way in. He knew her, and he said he wanted to talk. The flimsy bark walls of the hut weren't sufficient, she felt, to stop him from barging in, so she opened the door to him and tried to make the best of whatever discussion she could have with him about what he was after. They finished up in court as one of many such cases. The picture is of humpy life and was quite common in these parts.

I can cite, also, the story of a man called Dennis Kelly (I don't think he is one of Ned's relations) whose files I found in the Lands Department section of the State Archives in Melbourne. These Lands Department files contain extensive records of individual selectors and their correspondence with the department. Dennis Kelly's story fascinated me but it is not atypical. He took his selection of seventy-five acres at Seven Mile Creek in 1873 to supplement his earnings as a labourer. The first annual report half way through 1875 revealed that he had improved his selection to the tune of £10.4.0 by erecting four chains of post and rail fence, a two-roomed bark house (24 ft x 13 ft) and a piggery. The quality of the land, none of which was cultivated, was cold, wet and gravelly, 'poor soil fit for nothing but pasture'. About ten acres, he said, could be cultivated for one crop. He was using it to pasture seven cows, to help support his wife and seven children. He had been living on this block since 1868, and at last was going through the routine of selection. When they asked why he had not improved it sufficiently, he replied, 'If I fence off the creek, who will drive my cows to water? I am employed as a labourer around the district and my children are at school.' And he added that he had not been in full employment and had therefore been unable to pay his rent. The file records his sturdy endeavour to get this property going. In 1877, he had fifteen chains of fence, but still no cultivation. His hut was the same, but he had added a few sheds. Still he had trouble in paying his rent, and in a long series of pathetic letters Kelly told the lands people about the state of his purse. He hoped that the girls would soon be earning. Overall, nothing changed much, except for a bit of cultivation. The house was just as rickety right through.

In the end, after a long licence period, he obtained a lease. But, alas, a few years later his wife had to take over the lease because the poor man was dead. This is, in a way, typical of many cases of men living on the margin of pride and economics. And perhaps it is one of the reasons for larrikinism in this district. But larrikinism, an anti-philosophy of revolt, was not just a local phenomenon; it was typical of all society in this period. During the 1870s there was great concern about the teenager. I don't suppose that until recent times there has been a period when the teenager was so much under focus. These teenagers were the children of the generation of gold migrants. They had experienced movement from school to school, from goldfield to goldfield, with schoolmasters going off to the diggings, or doing the other curious things schoolmasters do when they give up their vocation. The larrikins were mainly an underprivileged group for whom the times had not been propitious. The education system was not overhauled until the 1870s, when it was too late for this group. They were given little education.

What I do not know about Ned Kelly, but what I suspect, on looking through the records, is that he had very little formal schooling. Instead, he shouldered the problems of supporting his family. Here was a basis of revolt; blind revolt against these conditions as well as against the oppressions (as Kelly saw them) of the police, and against the nature of law.

There are very human stories about poor men at this time, like that of the man who was found completely naked in the boiling sun, apparently having been there for a day or more. A routine police patrol discovered him unconscious on one of the back roads. He was making his way home to his selection after harvest work in the north and was trying to avoid the pubs along the main road. Apparently he had gone without food in order to take more money home, and had failed to keep himself in a fit condition. He survived. But with what marks of his experience?

It seems to me that in the hardships and hatreds of this

class there was a foundation for revolt. You may ask why didn't it become bigger in sympathy with Ned Kelly — well, I think that has something to do with Ned's individualism and pride. It would be instructive to know exactly what he thought he should be doing during the winter when he held the Jerilderie funds. The special nature of Ned Kelly's behaviour at Jerilderie over the mortgages and other deeds at the bank is very interesting because he acted as the representative of the small farmers by burning (even in New South Wales) any deeds that were an obstacle to the small man. The clerk at the bank was beside himself trying to persuade Ned not to burn his life insurance policy. But, as with the clergyman's watch, Ned handed over the policy. According to his actions, he was not interested in vandalism, but rather in a crusade in defence of little men. Real democracy, equality of conditions, did not exist; and in many ways, it seems to me, Kelly's attitude at Jerilderie expresses a groundswell of revolt. His actions were eloquent of a general sympathy with the poor, not just the poor of his own district.

Against these general social conditions we need to set the prevalence of horse stealing. The Royal Commission into the police gives interesting figures of something like a hundred cases of horse-stealing a year in the Beechworth Supreme Court area. Now I am not sure what this means. But I do think that the subject of horse-stealing in the Kelly area needs an extended investigation. Just how prevalent was it? What was its nature? Certainly a number of men, Ned Kelly among them, seem to have been in the business in a large way. But a single case of horse-stealing may not amount to a very serious thing. We accept a high incidence of car thefts in our community, for instance, and when the police tell us that 1967 is a record year for car thefts we are not surprised or particularly alarmed. Maybe much of the horse-stealing complained about was merely horse borrowing. Kelly probably began that way. The recovery figures are not stated. Therefore, what I suggested earlier about calamity-howling on the part of Chief Com missioner Standish, may have been paralleled in the concern of the propertied classes about horse-stealing, and their expressed desire to make even suspects suffer.

I must mention also the obvious gap in social conditions between the sophistication of towns like Beechworth, and the degradation of rural slums. To an aware person, to an angry person, this is something to be concerned about.

It is here, of course, that my final point about tradition comes in. The Irish tradition bred angry men. And I don't really need to add much to what Professor Manning Clark has said. Certainly Irish hatreds fed upon all these background conditions, and then erupted as I think they did at Eureka. Irish children were reminded of the past and present iniquities of the Anglo-Saxons. The Quinn family and the Kelly family seem to have been particularly strong institutions, particularly difficult to reject. So Ned, for instance, accepted a biased view of society. Why should he have rejected the views of his family when there was so much evidence before his eyes that the necessary revolt was against others? The Church doesn't seem to have greatly influenced Ned, and this interests me. I have read several accounts of the Roman Catholic situation in the north-east (statistical and otherwise) and with regard to the religious situation, here are some figures for the county of Delatite, the Kelly area. In 1881, county Delatite had 14,000 people, 5,000 of the Church of England and 2,000 Presbyterians, 1,400 Methodists, 332 other Protestants (which is a very low proportion, by the way, compared with the rest of the state) and 3,774 Catholics, some Roman, some not defined. The county had a slightly larger proportion of Catholics than the colony as a whole.

This is not striking. But I do think the question of Irish in the police that Ned raises is a very interesting one. I looked at the names of those who took part at Glenrowan: they do not suggest a preponderance of Irish, as the Stringybark murders do. The Stringybark case is fascinating for the fact that the police were all Irish. And this no doubt did something to Mr Kelly, who certainly held views about scabbing on your mates. He felt that these men were turning their backs on the Irish tradition of disrespect for authority. In fact they were scum, he says, because they were taking the government's money just to obtain a soft billet, as Fitzpatrick was.

Kelly also inhabited an area of tradition to which he seems to have been introduced by the bushranger Power. It involved a special *camaraderie* and as far as I can tell (and again this is a question that relates very strongly to the Kelly tradition) without any particular brutality or behaviour unbefitting a gentleman towards people other than the police. There is the famous case of the Euroa bank manager's wife who, whenever anyone behaved rudely in her presence, compared him unfavourably with Ned Kelly. This is consistent with the reports, already mentioned, of his behaviour at Jerilderie. I think we should raise in discussion just how much the attitude to Kelly in the area was related to the fact that although he may have talked big about what he would do to people who betrayed him, he did not in fact do anything along those lines. His war was with the police, and he tried to frighten those who might directly help them. That was why Curnow, the Glenrowan schoolteacher, *thought* that he was in trouble if Kelly found out what he was doing.

But what was the attitude to Kelly? This I can't really answer. I do think it possible that in the period from Jerilderie to Glenrowan he was already a myth. It is hard to say whether people believed sincerely that he might suddenly arrive and bail them up, or whether they were simply conspiring to heighten the drama of the intense legend he had already evoked. Certainly there were no examples of what he might do if they betrayed him. In the Kelly gang story there is only one 'fully paid up' betrayal. And the vengeance was exacted by Joe Byrne from his former great friend Aaron Sherritt in circumstances of a military character. It was not just revenge. And fair enough, that seems to be the point of his threat.

I hope I have supplied some workable explanations of

Ned Kelly in relation to his times. I have suggested that he is an expression of a phase in colonial development, a phase of land settlement, a phase of unrest after the gold rush, a phase of political jobbery and the distance between (the lack of understanding between) important groups in the community. I have suggested that he is to be understood in terms of the freedom and excitement of the horse, in contrast to the degraded conditions under which many people were living, and from which they could see no escape. He was a rare man, as Professor Manning Clark has said. He was both writer and man of action. He could have been famous rather than infamous. Naturally, I don't want you to think that I condone what he did. But to me it was a tremendous achievement. And those who were lesser men, those who had avoided the path of protest that led inevitably to the gallows, can be excused for making him a legend. In the peculiar circumstances of uncertain morality and a very materialist civilization, lesser men were entitled to think that Ned was a gentleman beside some of the land speculators who sent widows to the grave, and ruined thousands of investors. They were victims in many cases of lawful, but mostly of unlawful, activity, which the man of capital could usually get away with. The poor man has always been easier to nail. His reply was to make a hero of the man who was brave enough and bad enough to make war on society.

*Question:* Mr Bate, you were speaking of Mr Kelly's gentlemanliness — would his action towards the person he was shooting in cold blood be termed 'a gentleman's act'?
*Weston Bate:* I spoke of Mr Kelly having 'gentlemanly' attributes (and on the testimony of a woman witness). Would I describe the shooting of a policeman at Stringybark as gentlemanly? Well, let's face it, in Ned Kelly's eyes the police don't deserve gentlemanly treatment. So of course he is not gentlemanly in the way people behaved in Melbourne in those days. They would have issued writs

if they disagreed with someone. But Ned's view of the Stringybark incident was that the police were out to get him, and he accepted his role as an outlaw. Now was he an outlaw gentleman, or was he a ruffian outlaw? He believed that he was gentlemanly. 'I bailed them up,' he says, 'and gave them a chance to shoot.' Mind you, with his superb confidence, I am sure he reckoned to shoot first. I think it is true that they had rotten rifles and were unpractised in them (according to the Royal Commission). He was therefore vastly superior to them, and could afford to be gentlemanly enough to tell them to stand, which he says they wouldn't have done to him. But does that make him a gentleman? Well no, not according to us with collar and tie, and thoughts about gentlemen who don't smell under the armpits at dances, and that sort of thing. But on his own terms, I think, according to his own evidence (and we can't go anywhere else) he was as gentlemanly as he could be at that time. That is all the answer I can give to your very good question.

*Mr Phillips* [Yallourn]: What relative prospects did the Kelly family enjoy?

*Weston Bate:* We don't know, they didn't keep any account books. People in the ordinary line of business would have, but it is understood that Mrs Kelly ran a kind of — er — motel! along the highway. It is not recorded whether the Kellys were ever ungentlemanly enough to take their lodgers' horses. But the history of the Quinns is interesting, and that is that James Quinn had begun horse-stealing before the gold rush down Kilmore way and was able to buy the Glenmore station at the head of the King River. He was prominent in the 'horse-trading' business through to N.S.W. One of the findings of the Royal Commission in the early eighties was that the police should not have closed the police station at Glenmore right on the Quinns home stamping ground, because it was felt that this had kept down horse-stealing and kept them under surveillance. The way they lived was probably not related to the way the Kellys were living over at Greta, and I just don't know what money passed between them, or what were the profits of the horse-stealing racket. Ned, I know, was supposed to have been a past master at changing brands.

*Mrs A. Banfield* [Benalla]: I am rather surprised there hasn't yet come out of this discussion more reference as to why the Kelly legend still lives. I'd like to ask Mr Bate and the people here present whether they would agree that the social climate of the time, the kind of social government that existed in the colony at this time, would not lead people to use Ned Kelly's revolt as a symbol of what they one day hoped to see?

*Weston Bate:* I would like to go along with that. Yes, it is linked with my idea of the freedom that was conferred upon him by his tremendous skills, and his love of the horse. Social climate will always condition what people believe about the meaning of life, and the institution of Kelly as a legend clearly relates to the feelings of contemporaries and of people since. But I think what you have to explain is not just the beginning of the Kelly legend but also its continuation to this point in time. And obviously beyond this point. That to me has much more to do with the man than with society. The nostalgia of city-bound Australians is of course important. Not just the people of his own area felt sympathy with him, but also a whole tribe of urban Australians — even giggling city ladies (against their will, almost) thought of the great outback in terms of Kelly's Jerilderie raid. But his magnificence, and I think there is no other word for it, his skill in handling conditions, in handling his horses, is the key.

In those days everyone felt strongly about the way a man handled a horse (R.S.P.C.A. and all that). People believed that the horse was the noblest of animals. My view is that this tradition was nostalgically associated with Kelly by people living in cities. This man who, in Nolan's great pictures of him, is astride the world like a colossus. I think that is the basic reason for the legend. It was local, and at the time its importance related to social conditions. Later, just the quality of the man himself has appealed to all of us, though particularly in the context of city life.

*P. Clark* [Melbourne]: Mr Bate, I believe there is a considerable police dossier of evidence which any historian would be very pleased to get his hands on, and which might throw light on the whole subject, but which is unavailable. I don't know whether in the course of your researches you approached the police, and if so what answer you had?

*Weston Bate:* This is a terribly touchy subject. To me the Royal Commission at the time was most unsatisfactory, but it was Longmore's opportunity to get his own line across. There is a great tendency for Royal Commissions to be dominated by their Chairmen or by the strongest man in them. You ask people questions because you want certain kinds of answers, and you write up a report according to the way you like to think the evidence suggests things can be interpreted. That Royal Commission is to my mind a travesty. It throws quite a lot of light upon the police, but it probably confuses as much as it really enlightens us. And so I would share your anxiety to get hold of the material now that I have opened it up a bit myself. Perhaps there is somebody here who knows the right person, who could unlock it, and then, my word, if there is such a file the Kelly legend might burn again like the burning of the Glenrowan pub.

*Question:* Did the Ned Kelly incident lead to any action on the part of authority to put right the kind of grievances that might have been seen as causing the Kelly outbreak?

*Weston Bate:* No. The inquiry into the police, which I have suggested was a quaint thing in many ways, seems to me to have been a political enquiry, and not a social one at all. It cast some light on the social issues, but it wasn't occupying an ameliorative function at all, and it is perhaps interesting that there was no obvious social follow-up. This may make us reflect that perhaps the conditions weren't as strong as the Kellys thought they were, although you can produce evidence for degraded selectors, and many in these marginal areas, having a great deal of trouble to get on. There was a vast body of contented people to whom the lot of the unsuccessful was as nothing, and so the problem of the social protest is that Kelly represents a minority. Minorities have very little hope unless they are led by gifted spokesmen and persistent, and indeed violent, people. Protest seemed to go out with the passage of time when these people gave up their struggle and found that perhaps they could find employment in industries in country towns. Many ceased to care. They were disillusioned about the task of becoming independent landowners.

*Sgt. K. Holden* [Victorian Police, Public Relations]: I have been a very interested spectator of today's proceedings, with no original intention of rising to my feet. However, the question of the police file is one, I think, which should be answered, and can be quickly dealt with.

There is a great deal of the material available here. If anyone wishes, they may examine further files which I have with me, but which, I believe, do not contain anything of particular interest. The police file has been, for the last eight months, in the hands of the state archives and has been photostated for their use. At any time that they require facts, they are always welcome to have the file. There is nothing in it which condemns or congratulates the Police on the handling of the Kelly episode.

*R. Beazley* [Wangaratta]: This is more in the nature of a comment than a question. First, the comment on sheep-stealing, horse-stealing and cattle-stealing, and the indignation of the local people of that time to these crimes. Weston Bate referred to the Benalla magistrate, for instance, who fined people five pounds for stealing sheep. It was then, and still is, a serious crime on the statute books. It is still punishable by up to ten years' jail. As recently as last month, I was with a judge here in Wangaratta who said that he was compelled to sentence a particular person convicted of sheep-stealing to two years' jail. This, I believe, is because the livelihood of the people in this area, now as then, depends greatly upon sheep and horses. So perhaps the indignation of the people on that count was to be expected at that time.

Secondly, Mr Bate commented upon the decentralization of authority and the question of who was running the country at that time. During the past few weeks, prompted by the notice of this particular symposium, an investigation was made of the local record books of the Wangaratta Court House, which date back quite a long way. What was revealed was that, in 1871, when Kelly was only sixteen years of age, he was charged with receiving a horse which was known to have been stolen. This was in regard to the affair with 'Wild' Wright, whom the record named as Isiah Wright.

Kelly was first brought to the Court in Wangaratta before a local Justice of the Peace. He was remanded for a week. The record shows that, in the margin, the Justice of the Peace wrote: 'I am most unwilling to bail this prisoner'. At this time, Kelly's prior convictions were of a very minor nature.

The following week, he was arraigned before the court again — having been in custody all this time — and the magistrate, after hearing the police application for an adjournment to consider the matter further, also wrote in the margin: 'This prisoner should not be bailed'.

One presumes that the magistrate had already read the previous notation by the Justice of the Peace, who was a local identity, presumably a 'landed gentleman', though no one seems to know.

As a result of this, Kelly was not granted bail. He presumably spent three months in prison before he was brought before the Court at Beechworth in August of that year. Perhaps this helps us to understand why he was so antagonistic towards authority. I do not know of anyone here who has seen these records, because, as far as we knew, they did not exist before we, more or less accidentally, came across them.

*Weston Bate:* I'd like to applaud that announcement, anyway. [*Applause.*] As a 'city boy' myself, the question of sheep-stealing has worried me. Sheep-stealing seems to have been very serious, and this was the point of my statement. The magistrate's decision in the case you have cited indicates that the mere suggestion that these people were horse-stealers or sheep-stealers was enough to warrant them special treatment.

Kelly, certainly in his Jerilderie Letter, indicates that he had a great backlog of this kind of experience in his heart. The fact that he was not bailed then seems to me to lead to the Fitzpatrick case, to give us some indication of Kelly's relations with the law. Professor Waller will be dealing with Kelly's trial later, but there is the much larger issue of what the law was up to, and what side the law was on.

You see, right from the early seventies and Kelly's association with Power, there was a blanket provision in the district that these fellows at Greta were dangerous. 'We can't easily pin these things on them,' we can hear it said, 'but we'll get 'em. We'll get 'em all right.' The moment they stepped out of line, they were given superior treatment, even to being sent to Pentridge, as Ned found later, for a crime which was not, apparently, nearly commensurate with the punishment meted out.

It's pretty clear that, whatever his story, Ned Kelly did 'receive' the horse from Wright. But, as it was pointed out, the fellows who actually stole the horse got their eighteen months and Ned got three years. It was the 'Greta Mob' which was in the consciousness of the law, and it was determined to deal with them, legally or otherwise.

*Statement* [from the floor]: I have lived in Glenrowan for many years and, of course, I have heard many, many stories. I am interested in your statement about the Kellys being hunted by the law. Although stories may conflict, one thing I do know: Jim Kelly, the youngest brother, was one of the most beloved men in the whole of the district. He would help anybody that was down, or wanted help. At any time, he would help.

*Weston Bate:* May I ask you a question, then? Is there any clarity of accusation the other way? That is, about rough treatment or threats by the gang, or the kind of suggestion Curnow makes? Of course, if one wishes to take the gentlemanliness of Ned to extremes, Curnow's attitude may be seen as that of the alien schoolteacher not understanding or sympathizing with the local traditions and so on; putting his own construction on, or even distorting the facts of, what happened. We don't know. Professor Manning Clark was prepared to accept the honesty of Curnow, I know, but I wonder whether there are indications of people being really frightened by the Kellys, in the sense that there would follow sharp and summary action should they not do what the Kellys wanted. Or is it too confused by legend now?

*Answer:* I do not think that any of the people in the district were ever frightened of any of the Kellys.

## 3

# The Kellys and Beechworth

IAN JONES

*Ian Jones is a former journalist and a television producer-director currently working on a film on Ned Kelly. As a director for Crawford Productions and Pegasus Productions he has been associated with Australian Films and television programmes.*

*A student of Kelly history for almost forty years, he has combined formal research with extensive fieldwork among the people of the Kelly country.*

The Kellys, all of them, were well-known figures in the streets of Beechworth, because Beechworth was virtually the capital of the north-east. You'll find maps still being printed overseas which show only four towns in Victoria — Melbourne, Geelong, Ballarat and Beechworth. This was one of the major centres of the State and on Boxing Day, coachloads, and later, trainloads of people travelled 170 miles from Melbourne to attend the festivities at Beechworth. The town's Prince of Wales Birthday procession was famous not only throughout the State, but throughout Australia.

Ned Kelly was often seen in Beechworth, as was Kate Kelly, his sister. She was, strangely enough, a close friend of Emma Crawford, daughter of Beechworth's millionaire coaching magnate, Hiram Crawford. Possibly through this friendship with Emma Crawford Kate Kelly first met Aaron Sherritt. It is not generally known that Aaron Sherritt and Kate Kelly were, at one time, sweethearts. The romance broke off and was resumed in rather unusual circumstances during the Kelly outbreak.

One member of the gang, Steve Hart, was born in the Beechworth district. It is generally believed that he was born at Wangaratta in 1860, but he was actually born at Beechworth in 1859.

However, the main link of Beechworth with the Kelly gang is through two men, Joe Byrne and Aaron Sherritt. Joe is supposed to have been born at Beechworth in 1857. There is no proof of this but we do know that shortly after this date his family was living on the Woolshed, some nine miles from Beechworth. Joe's father was a digger called Paddy Byrne, who had come out here with other members of his family during the Irish potato famine in the 1840s. Also in Beechworth at this period lived the Sherritt family. Father of the family was John Sherritt, who had been a member of the hated Constabulary in Ireland. He was also an Orangeman. From the start, the Sherritts were bound to be unpopular with their predominantly Irish neighbours.

Joe Byrne and Aaron Sherritt became friends at the Woolshed School. Joe was a smart lad, well liked by his teacher. Aaron was not so smart apparently, or perhaps he just did not care. Joe became a bush poet. He could write passable parodies and doggerel. Aaron reached adult life barely able to sign his name. Yet the two boys became close friends. It was a rather unholy alliance. They got into all sorts of scraps. However people were fairly tolerant of them on the whole.

In 1870, Joe's father died, fitting the pattern that Weston Bate showed us yesterday — a man battling to make a living for his family, on the tail end of a gold rush, working as a digger, a bullock driver, a carrier, a dairy farmer; trying digging again, and eventually dying of heart disease in his mid-thirties. Mrs Byrne was left three months pregnant, with seven children, the eldest only fourteen. Joe, at this stage, was capable of earning a living, but did little to help. He worked for a while at the Beechworth tannery, but spent most of his time vagabonding around the district with his mate Aaron Sherritt.

Soon, Aaron took up a selection of 107 acres — quite a large holding for this part of the country — and Joe and Aaron spent some time working on it. Somehow, Joe met Ned Kelly. Joe's sister told me shortly before her death, in 1964, that while Joe and Aaron were serving a six months' sentence for being found in possession of a supposedly stolen cow hide, they met Jim Kelly. On the day Joe was released from prison, Jim asked him the quickest way to Greta, and Joe is supposed to have said, 'I'll show you the way.' Not being in any particular hurry to get home and face a rather embarrassing scene with the family, he rode to Greta with Jim Kelly and, supposedly, there met Ned.

Certainly, by the late 1870s, Ned Kelly and Joe Byrne were close friends. They were a striking pair. Both were particularly good-looking, well-dressed young men. Both were boxing enthusiasts, so dedicated to the sport that they risked capture during their outlawry to watch the famous Larry Foley-Jed Mace fight at Echuca. Both, incidentally, had broken noses.

Joe and Ned easily passed themselves off as young squatters — a guise they used in their favourite horse-stealing technique. Joe, Ned, Aaron Sherritt, Dan Kelly and possibly Steve Hart, would steal a mob of horses. Ned and Joe would then separate, each taking one of the other boys with him. Joe and Ned would dress well, ride the best horses. Their mates would dress as stockmen. Ned would ride up to a property, perhaps in the Riverina, and ask if he could put up a couple of his horses for the night. The station owner was probably delighted to have company. Shortly afterwards the second member of the act would arrive. Joe would come riding up, and would admire one of Ned's horses (which, of course, they had previously stolen). The squatter would then be only too happy to witness a transaction in which Joe Byrne 'bought' this horse from Ned Kelly. The transaction was duly recorded on the squatter's notepaper, and they then had a legal bill of sale for a stolen horse. This was a spectacularly successful ruse which the Kellys pulled off many times. The climax, of course, was to take the horses down to the great mecca of the horsy set, Kirk's Bazaar, Melbourne, still masquerading as young squatters, get a handsome price for them and then 'paint Bourke red'.

With the battle at Stringybark Creek in 1878, Ned Kelly, Dan Kelly, Joe Byrne and Steve Hart became outlaws. It just happened that Joe and Steve were with Ned and Dan Kelly at that time. It could quite easily have been Aaron Sherritt. It could have been Tom Lloyd, or Denny McAuliffe, or Wild Wright, or Jack McEvoy, or John O'Brien, or Joe Havey, or any of their close friends.

Aaron Sherritt had an incredible admiration for Ned Kelly — admiration which approached hero-worship. Aaron was bitter that he was not included in the gang. Apparently Ned tried to make it clear that no gang had been formed, that these men were fugitives and he was going to help them stay outside the law. Tom Lloyd, Ned's cousin, who helped the gang throughout their outlawry, never became a member of the gang as such. However, Aaron Sherritt must have been conscious that he was always slightly on the outside. Because he was an Orangeman, because he was a Protestant, he was always suspect by the Catholic Irish.

Aaron remained on the fringe of the group, yet he had this enormously close friendship with Joe Byrne. Perhaps he was bitter about what he could feel to be his rejection by Ned Kelly. Nevertheless, he scouted for the gang in their dash to the flooded Murray and back. The police conducted the so-called 'Charge of Sebastopol' on the Sherritt homestead, acting days late on a report that the Kellys had been seen there. They subsequently raided the Byrne homestead and Aaron Sherritt appeared there. (While Joe was away, Aaron often used to go there to cut wood and help Mrs Byrne around the property.) At this stage he was engaged to Joe Byrne's sister. Sherritt was approached there and then to become a police spy. He accepted.

This is the great enigma of the Kelly story — the so-called betrayal of the gang by Aaron Sherritt.

For nearly ninety years people have never doubted that Aaron Sherritt actively betrayed the Kelly gang, yet if we look at the evidence closely — and there is a mass of material provided in books by police officers, in police documents, and in tens of thousands of questions in the Minutes of Evidence of the Royal Commission — we are forced to conclude that Sherritt did not actually betray the gang. Sherritt was working as a double agent and was accepting money from the police. But the picture one forms is that he was actually helping to keep the police away from the gang. Superintendent Hare placed considerable trust in Sherritt. Detective Ward, stationed at Beechworth, was wary of Sherritt, but felt he could be of some use.

Sherritt's greatest value to the police was in providing a line of action — an opportunity to do something — at a time when there seemed no possible plan to pursue, and when political pressure and public opinion demanded action.

Sherritt was willing to lead the police on absurd watch parties. He was willing to make fools of them, camping them in a cave miles from the Byrne homestead, leading them every day on a nightmare scramble across rocks and gullies and ti-tree thickets to a spot a mile from the Byrne homestead, where they sat all day in rain and shine to watch for the Kelly gang. There was a perfectly good cave a little way up the range from the Byrne homestead which had been used by the gang shortly after the Stringybark Creek murders, a cave which Aaron Sherritt knew about. On the range, directly above the Byrne homestead, was a perfectly good lookout point from which the police could have looked straight into Mrs Byrne's front window with a powerful telescope. But Sherritt didn't take the police there. Sherritt earned his money and kept his own strange peace.

On one memorable occasion a police party was watching the Byrne homestead at night. Aaron Sherritt had visited his fiancée, Joe Byrne's sister. Superintendent Hare was with the party, hiding under a brush and rail fence around the old Byrne stockyard, when suddenly a figure approached from the ranges. Joe Byrne walked with what was described as 'a peculiar swagger' — with an exaggerated backswing of the right arm. This unusual walk was immediately recognized by a couple of troopers who knew him. Hare signalled the men to do nothing and they held their positions. Joe Byrne walked down through the stockyard, climbed over the fence behind which Hare was hiding, and entered the Byrne homestead where Aaron Sherritt was visiting his fiancée and, of course, Mrs Byrne and the other children.

Hours passed. Eventually the police crept up to the homestead, but only the Byrne family and Sherritt were there. Hare confronted Sherritt with this, asking, 'What happened to Joe Byrne?' Sherritt answered, 'I don't know what you are talking about.' Hare said, 'Who was that fellow who came here?' Sherritt replied, 'That was a fellow called Scotty who lives up on the Ranges.' Hare said, 'Where did he go?' Sherritt answered, 'He just went out the back way.'

There can be little doubt that, on this occasion at least, Sherritt deliberately helped Joe Byrne evade capture by the police. In doing so, he let £2,000 slip happily through his fingers.

The logical question is: 'Why did Joe Byrne kill Aaron Sherritt if Aaron Sherritt did not in fact betray the Kelly gang?' And this is quite a question. It is a very complex problem and one I can barely do justice to in the time at our disposal. Basically, a situation had developed in which the relationship between Joe Byrne and Aaron Sherritt was resented bitterly by both their families. There was a dangerous relationship between Aaron and Detective Ward, who was a leader of this aspect of the Kelly pursuit at Beechworth. It was mentioned in the Royal Commission and has been acknowledged by district and family tradition that Detective Ward had seduced Aaron Sherritt's fiancée. Oddly enough one would think that Sherritt's feeling to

Ward would be rather stronger than Ward's feeling to Sherritt. This, apparently, was not the case. Perhaps Ward regarded Sherritt as a dangerous man who was biding his time for revenge. Whatever the cause, Ward was out to get Sherritt. There is ample evidence in the Royal Commission minutes on this point. One is led to the inescapable conclusion that Ward was trying to set Aaron Sherritt up as bait to bring the Kelly gang out of hiding.

Ward arranged for a saddle to be stolen from Aaron Sherritt's wife. (I should explain Sherritt's marriage here: Mrs Byrne found Aaron Sherritt in a police camp one morning, and made her daughter break off their engagement. Aaron then gleefully paid court to Kate Kelly, but this romance was nipped in the bud by Margaret Skillion, Kate's elder sister. So, the irrepressible Aaron then wooed and wedded a Woolshed girl, Ellen Barry, in a matter of two months.) A saddle was stolen from Aaron's wife and planted in the Byrne homestead. Evidence on this point is unequivocal, and the hand of Detective Ward is clearly upon the whole thing.

Shortly after this came the remarkable business of the police being established in Sherritt's hut, allegedly to guard Sherritt. This is nonsense. If anything, Sherritt was guarding the police. The police were actually billeted in Sherritt's hut to watch the Byrne homestead. They would camp there by day, and each night Sherritt would lead them across the creek and along its banks to the Byrne homestead, where they would squat in the freezing grass all night. Then, at dawn, Aaron would lead them back to his hut. The police would sleep all day, and go out again the following night. Aaron's brother pointed out to the Royal Commission that the police, guided by Aaron, had been watching the front of the Byrne homestead. Between their position and the homestead ran a deep mining race, along which, he said, half a dozen men could have passed without anybody seeing them. Aaron Sherritt knew perfectly well that the mining race was there and, of course, that this was the path Joe normally followed to the homestead when visiting his mother. Aaron also insisted that he was always with the police while they were watching the homestead. He wanted to make sure that nothing went wrong.

However, during the early months of 1880, the position was growing completely out of hand. Sherritt was living in a kind of fantasy world. He was acknowledged as a traitor by many people in the Beechworth district. He was a dangerous man, a formidable bare-knuckle fighter, and no one seems to have made direct threats against him. He openly acknowledged that the only man he had ever been scared of was Ned Kelly. However, this double life was slowly catching up with Sherritt; this strange deception was beginning to sap his nerve. And Joe, who had believed in Aaron's fidelity all along, was beginning to have doubts. Joe's own family were coming to him with stories — stories of the saddle, stories of vile threats which Aaron was supposed to have made against Joe. These stories are effectively refuted by the sworn evidence of the police who were living with Sherritt at this time. They pointed out that they did not think Sherritt was really helping them as he was always boasting about what his mate, Joe Byrne, was going to do, and how useless it was to chase the Kelly gang because they would never catch them. But to the minds of hunted and suspicious men, the threads of evidence against Sherritt were forming a pattern.

There is a mysterious incident in the week before Glenrowan. We have an account of a meeting between Aaron Sherritt and a trooper, followed by a pub crawl during which the trooper tried to get the truth from Sherritt as to whether he was or was not true to the police. Eventually, they visited a hotel where Joe's girlfriend worked as a barmaid. As they entered, the girl was kissing a digger. Aaron was apparently disgusted. He told the trooper that this was Joe Byrne's girlfriend and stalked out of the pub in high dudgeon.

The trooper, showing great presence of mind, immediately walked up to the girl and took her to the Beechworth Police Station for questioning. She, of course, realized exactly what had happened. The tradition is that this incident occurred on the Thursday, and Aaron Sherritt was shot on the Saturday. I do not believe it was quite as simple as that, but some culminating incident of this kind could well have led up to this final decision to shoot Aaron Sherritt — this final refusal to go along any more in the atmosphere of doubt and suspicion.

So you have the keystone of the Glenrowan campaign created by the murder of Aaron Sherritt. This was the last part played by Beechworth in the actual exploits of the gang.

On the evening of 26 June, Joe Byrne and Dan Kelly bailed up Anton Wicks and took him to the door of Sherritt's hut in the Woolshed, where Sherritt was sitting by the fire with his pregnant bride and his mother-in-law. Four police sat in the next room playing cards. There was that fateful knock. Aaron opened the door, started to crack a joke — typically Sherritt — and a shotgun blasted twice from the darkness. One bullet struck him in the throat just above the collarbone and the second in the stomach just above the navel. He died almost immediately. And the trap was sprung. The whole mad Glenrowan campaign was pinnacling towards this ghastly Armageddon that faced the gang.

Beechworth's last direct link with the gang was, of course, when Ned was brought there for his preliminary trial. The trial began in the Beechworth Court House, quaintly enough, with the Chief Commissioner of Police sitting beside the magistrate. However, it was decided that the trial proper would not be conducted in Beechworth because 'of the impossibility of finding an impartial jury'. In point of fact, of course, it would not be possible to find a jury to convict Ned Kelly in Beechworth, whether the cause be direct sympathy or fear of retaliation from the sympathizers. So Ned was hustled out of Beechworth and taken down to Melbourne, where he was tried and executed.

Feeling in Beechworth is still strong about the Kelly business, particularly the Byrne and Sherritt links. The

Byrne family left Beechworth almost immediately after the death of Joe. They moved to Albury, not because they were ashamed, but because they wanted to forget about the whole wretched incident. Mrs Byrne, a brave little woman, decent and hard-working, raised her seven children, scraping together a living as best she could with the help of her two surviving sons. Members of the Sherritt family still live around Beechworth. I know some of them well. Their feeling toward Aaron is strange. They believe, with most other people, that he betrayed the gang, that he was a traitor and died a traitor's death.

One of the saddest things I had seen in a long time was the unmarked grave of Aaron Sherritt in the Beechworth cemetery. But a much sadder sight awaited me when I traced the grave of Aaron's father. I discovered that, twenty years after Aaron's death, John Sherritt, quite a successful and well-respected farmer in the district, chose to be buried in an unmarked grave simply so that he could lie beside his son.

The thesis that Aaron did not betray the gang has already proved unpopular. However, while I hesitate to be dogmatic, I honestly feel that a critical evaluation of all available evidence fails to prove that Sherritt ever did one thing to bring the police pursuit any closer to the Kelly gang.

*Peter Clark* [Melbourne]: Have you any theories about Kate Kelly's rejection by Aaron Sherritt as being a factor in Sherritt's death at the hands of the gang?

*Ian Jones:* I don't think it was a rejection of Kate. As I say, the indications are that he met Kate via Emma Crawford, whose father was a partner in the coaching firm of Crawford and Connelly. After a tragic beginning on the goldfields, Hiram Crawford became virtually a millionaire, built a magnificent arcade in Melbourne and had this successful coaching company. Now, Kate and Emma's friendship was an unlikely one, but it was there. Emma Crawford, I might add, bought Aaron's selection from him. They knew one another quite well. I do not think there is any suggestion that Aaron rejected Kate. The fact that Kate seemed happy to resume the relationship probably indicates that they had parted friends.

When Mrs Byrne made Kate Byrne break off the engagement Aaron went after Kate Kelly again; Maggie Skillion forestalled this by swearing a charge of horse-stealing against Aaron. Aaron was probably quite fond of Kate. As a matter of fact there is a letter from Joe Byrne to Aaron in which he refers to the fact that one night when Aaron had visited Kate, the gang arrived shortly afterwards and followed him to try and overtake him.

*Peter Clark* [Melbourne]: One gets the impression that Kate had some set against men in general, that someone had dealt her a bitter blow sometime or another. Maybe Kate used her influence with her brother?

*Ian Jones:* Kate emerges as a rather different kind of figure from what you might imagine. She was a wonderful horse-woman, of course, who used to ride bare-back with her arms around the horse's neck. She used to ride astride, too, which was considered rather eccentric.

Apart from this, she emerges as a rather quiet, shy girl. This is revealed in many ways, including a very good police description by Detective Ward.

In an unpublished manuscript in my possession, there is a description of a meeting between Kate Kelly and Constable Fitzpatrick in September 1877. There are indications that there had been a mild flirtation between the two at the time when Fitzpatrick was a friend of Ned's. This may lend something to the story that Fitzpatrick made some advance to Kate which triggered off the Fitzpatrick incident. The story is consistent. A descendant of the Kelly family showed me the exact spot in the Kelly kitchen where Fitzpatrick was supposed to have been sitting on a form when Kate walked into the kitchen. He supposedly caught her by the waist and pulled her on to his lap, something which might not have offended Kate terribly, but which Dan did not take very well.

# Kelly — The Folk-Hero

### A RECITAL by
### IAN JONES and GLEN TOMASETTI

*Ian Jones:* I sometimes wonder what people mean by 'the legend of Ned Kelly'. The phrase has often indicated, I believe, a lack of concern with what really happened. We may find that the Kelly story itself has the quality and stature of legend.

First, then, some descriptions of Ned Kelly. Here are the opinions of two of his super-enemies.

Long before Sergeant Steele's last fight with Ned Kelly, at a time when he was simply a police officer anxious to apprehend Kelly on a charge of horse-stealing, Steele said simply: 'Edward Kelly is a man about six feet, dark complexioned, dark moustache, almond-shaped eyes, dark brown whiskers and hair. A raw bony man.'

We have a different type of description from Constable Fitzpatrick who probably perjured himself over those cloudy incidents of 15 April 1878; whose career in the police force was destroyed because of his involvement in those mysterious events, and who went through life with the blight of his association with the Kellys hanging over his head. He said, in 1911, thirty-one years later:

Ned Kelly rises before me as I speak. Considering his environment, he was a superior man. He possessed great natural ability, and, under favourable circumstances, would probably have become a leader of men in good society instead of the head of a gang of outlaws.

Finally, the opinion of a man who admired Ned to the point almost of worship. Jon Robitt Clow says:

> In the Kellian country, there were not the facilities for a Charlemagne, nor the need for a Washington, but Providence assigned to our General the task of resisting that low estimation the European placed upon the native-born and to affirm that we have an individuality of our own making that is not to be trifled with. No matter what his faults were, he is the father of our national courage and the heart of our literature.

Many years after Mr Clow wrote those words, a writer, Max Brown, searched for the truth of the Kelly story — far more successfully than many who went before or who have come after. In the Foreword to his book *Australian Son,* which is in many ways the best biography of Ned Kelly ever written, he said:

> Out of rain or sun in spacious stables dead with the smell of dust and benzine and incongruous with sleek, beetle-shaped automobiles, I have seen the wooden stalls as they were, each with its mount. I have heard them whinny and champ in the night. I have seen again the days when the iron horse was advancing but still the horse was king, when benzine was hay, the service station the farrier's forge, the days when the flasher your horse and the flasher your gear, the damn sight flasher you were.
>
> But dream as I can in the shadow of the Alps where these four young bushmen rode, I shall never savour the tang of their voices, hear them laugh or curse, feel with my hand against their hearts, the impact of the first great disaster, of their summer triumphs when the electric telegraph flung their deeds across the world, of the days of waiting, of boredom — the black days of decay and futility towards the end — and of the final desperate lunge to revenge themselves on the police claw of official-

dom which they never ceased to contend had harried them without just cause.

*Glen Tomasetti:*

KELLY WAS THEIR CAPTAIN

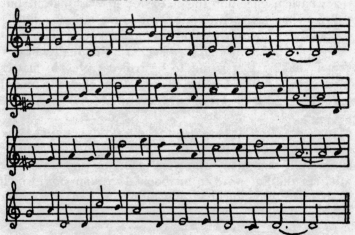

Come all you wild colonial boys and attention to me pay,
While in my song I do unfold the truth without delay,
'Tis of a famous outlawed band that roamed this country round,
Ned Kelly was their captain, no better could be found.

And though they deemed them outlaws, brave men they proved to be,
And vengeance ranked in every breast for Kelly's misery,
They burned his mother's vine-clad hut, which caused his heart to yearn,
And angered his companions, Steve Hart and brave Jo Byrne.

One day as Ned and his comrades in ambush lay concealed,
They spied three mounted troopers and their presence did reveal,
He called to them 'Surrender'. These words to them he said,
'Resist a man amongst you and I'll surely shoot you dead.'

Now Kennedy, Scanlon and Lonigan in death were lying
    low,
When Ned amongst them recognized his old and vicious
    foe,
He thought him of his mother with a baby at her breast,
It filled his heart with anger and the country knows the
    rest.

It was in the Wombat Ranges Ned Kelly made his haunt,
And all those Victorian troopers at his name did truly
    daunt,
For months they lay in ambush until finally betrayed
By the traitor Aaron Sherritt. His life that treachery paid.

'Twas at Glenrowan station the conflict raged severe,
When more than fifty policemen at the scene did then
    appear,
No credit to their bravery, no credit to their name,
Ned Kelly terrified them all and put their blood to shame.

[Abridged from Stewart and Keesing, *Old Bush Songs*
(Sydney, 1957). Sung unaccompanied to the tune of 'The
Death of Ben Hall.' *Penguin Australian Songbook* (1964).]

*Ian Jones:* Ned Kelly was an Irishman. To approach this
fact is to approach his legend. From the Jerilderie Letter,
then, a passage which has already been quoted in part by
Professor Manning Clark in the opening paper. I think it
shows the fire, the passion, the reality of the past as it lived
in Ned Kelly.

Kelly spoke in what has been described as a 'clear, ring-
ing brogue':

What would people say if they saw a strapping big lump
of an Irishman shepherding sheep for fifteen bob a week
or tailing turkeys in Tallarook ranges for a smile from
Julia or even begging his tucker, they would say he ought
to be ashamed of himself and tar-and-feather him. But
he would be a king to a policeman who for a lazing loaf-
ing cowardly bilit left the ash corner deserted the shamrock, the emblem of true wit and beauty to serve under

77

a flag and nation that has destroyed massacred and murdered their fore-fathers by the greatest of torture as rolling them down hill in spiked barrels pulling their toe and finger nails and on the wheel and every torture imaginable more was transported to Van Diemand's Land to pine their young lives away in starvation and misery among tyrants worse than the promised hell itself all of true blood bone and beauty and that was not murdered on their own soil, or had fled to America or other countries to bloom again another day were doomed to Port McQuarie Toweringabbie Norfolk island and Emu plains and in those places of tyrany and condemnation many a blooming Irishman rather than subdue to the Saxon yoke were flogged to death and bravely died in servile chains but true to the shamrock and a credit to Paddys land What would people say if I became a policeman and took an oath to arrest my brothers and sisters and relations and convict them by fair or foul means after the conviction of my mother and the persecutions and insults offered to myself and people Would they say I was a decent gentleman and yet a policeman is still in worse and guilty of meaner actions than than The Queen must surely be proud of such heroic men as the Police and Irish soldiers as It takes eight or eleven of the biggest mud crushers in Melbourne to take one poor little half starved larrakin to a watchhouse. I have seen as many as eleven, big and ugly enough to lift Mount Macedon out of a crab hole more like the species of a baboon or Guerilla than a man actually come into a court house and swear they could not arrest one eight stone larrakin and then armed with battens and niddies without some civilians assistance and some of them going to the hospital from the effects of hits from the fists of the larrakin and the Magistrate would send the poor little larrakin into a dungeon for being a better man than such a parcel of armed curs. What would England do if America declared war and hoisted a green flag as it is all Irishman that has got command of her armies forts and batteries even her very life guards and beef tasters are Irish would they not slew around and fight her with their own arms for the sake of the colour they dare not wear for years and to reinstate it and rise old Erins isle once more from the pressure and tyrannism of the English yoke which has kept it in poverty and starvation and caused them to wear the enemy's coat. What else can England expect.

We have already spoken of Ned Kelly's devotion to his family, his mother, his sisters. Briefly, we have encountered Kate Kelly. Here, then, is a comparatively unemotional and accurate description of Kate by a detective:

> Kate Kelly, age about eighteen years, five feet four inches high, slender built, dark complexion and hair, thin features, dark piercing eyes, very small chain, fairly good looking, and reserved manner. When in Victoria, generally dresses in dark clothes.

Anything but unemotional (and possibly accurate) is this description by Ned Kelly in the Jerilderie Letter of police raids carried out on the Kelly homestead while he and Dan were away and Jim Kelly was in prison:

> I heard how the police used to be blowing that they would not ask me to stand they would shoot me first and then cry surrender and how they used to rush into the house upset all the milk dishes break tins of eggs empty the flour out of bags onto the ground and even the meat out of the cask and destroy all the provisions and shove the girls in front of them into the rooms like dogs so as if anyone was there they would shoot the girls first but they knew well I was not there or I would have scattered their blood and brains like rain. I would manure the Eleven Mile with their bloated carcasses and yet remember there is not one drop of murderous blood in my veins.
>
> Superintendent Smith used to say to my sisters see all the men I have out today I will have as many more tomorrow and we will blow him into pieces as small as

79

paper that is in our guns Detective Ward and Constable Hayes took out their revolvers and threatened to shoot the girls and children in Mrs. Skillians absence the greatest ruffians and murderers no matter how depraved would not be guilty of such a cowardly action, and this sort of cruelty and disgraceful and cowardly conduct to my brothers and sisters who had no protection coupled with the conviction of my mother and those men certainly made my block boil and I don't think there is a man born could have the patience to suffer it as long as I did or ever allow his blood to get cold while such insults as these were unavenged and yet in every paper that is printed I am called the blackest and coldest blooded murderer ever on record.

*Glen Tomasetti:* Ned Kelly's farewell to Greta when he went into the Wombat ranges:

### NED KELLY'S FAREWELL TO GRETA

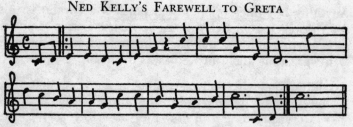

Farewell to home in Greta, my sister Kate farewell;
It grieves my heart to leave you, but here I cannot dwell.
The brand of Cain is on my brow, the bloodhounds on my trail,
And for the sake of golden gain my freedom they assail.
But should they cross my chequered path, by all I hold on earth,
I'll give them cause to rue the day their mothers gave them birth.
I'll shoot them down like kangaroos that roam the forests wide,
And leave their bodies bleaching upon some woodland side.

Oh Edward dearest brother, you know you cannot go
And risk to be encountered by such a mighty foe!
It's duly North lies Morgan's Tower, and pointing to the
sky,
South-east and East the mighty range of Gippsland moun-
tains lie.
You know the country well, dear Ned, go take your
comrades there
Where you may live as freely as the wombat and the bear,
And let no petty quarrels part the union of our gang,
But stick to one another, Ned, and guard our brother Dan.

[Collected by the Folk Lore Society of Victoria from Mrs Petie
of Brunswick, Melbourne. Also collected by Max Brown in
Beechworth and said to be sung about 1879. From *Penguin
Australian Songbook* (1964).]

*Ian Jones:* Here now is the Stringybark Creek gun-battle as
described by Ned Kelly himself, again from the Jerilderie
Letter:

I wasn't in the Wombat Ranges long and on the 25th
October I came on Police tracks between Table top and
the bogs. I crossed them and returning in the evening
I came on a different lot of tracks making for the shingle
hut I went to our camp and told my brother and his two
mates, me and my brother went and found their camp
at the shingle hut about a mile from my brothers house.
We saw they carried long firearms and we knew our
doom was sealed if we could not beat those before the
others would come as I knew the other part of Police
would soon join them and if they came on us at our camp
they would shoot us down like dogs at our work as we
had only two guns we thought it best to try and bail
those up, take their firearms and ammunition and horses
and we could stand a chance with the rest. We
approached the spring as close as we could get to the
camp as the intervening space being clear ground and

81

no battery we saw two men at the logs they got up and one took a double barreled fowling piece and fetched a horse down and hobbled him at the tent we thought there were more men in the tent asleep those outside being on sentry we could have shot those two men without speaking but not wishing to take their lives we waited. McIntyre laid his gun against a stump and Lonigan sat on the log I advanced, my brother Dan keeping McIntyre covered which he took to be Constable Flood and had he not obeyed my orders, or attempted to reach for the gun or draw his revolver he would have been shot dead, but when I called on them to throw up their hands McIntyre obeyed and Lonigan ran some six or seven yards to a battery of logs instead of dropping behind the one he was sitting on, he had just got to the logs and put his head up to take aim when I shot him that instant or he would have shot me.

As soon as I shot Lonigan he jumped up and staggered some distance from the logs with his hands raised and then fell he surrendered but too late I asked McIntyre who was in the tent he replied no one. I advanced and took possession of their two revolvers and fowling piece which I loaded with bullets instead of shot.

I asked McIntyre where his mates was he said they had gone down the creek and he did not expect them that night he asked me was I going to shoot him and his mates. I told him no I would shoot no man if he gave up his arms and leave the force he said the police all knew Fitzpatrick had wronged us and he intended to leave the force as he had bad health and his life was insured he told me he intended going home and that Kennedy and Scanlon were out looking for our camp and also about the other Police he told me the N.S.W. police had shot a man for shooting Sergeant Wallings. I told him if they did they had shot the wrong man and I expect your gang came to do the same with me he said no they did not come to shoot me they came to apprehend me I asked him what they carried spencer rifles and breech loading fowling pieces and so much ammunition for as the police was only supposed to carry one revolver and six cartridges in the revolver but they had eighteen rounds of revolver cartridges each three dozen for the fowling piece and twenty-one spencer rifle cartridges and God knows how many they had away with the rifle this looked as if they meant not only to shoot me but to riddle me but I don't know either Kennedy Scanlon or him and had nothing against them, he said he would get them to give up their arms if I would not shoot them as I could not blame them, they had to do their duty I said I did not blame them for doing honest duty but I could not suffer them blowing me to pieces in my own native land and they knew Fitzpatrick wronged us and why not make it public and convict him but no they would rather riddle poor unfortunate creoles, but they will rue the day ever Fitzpatrick got among them. Our two mates came over when they heard the shot fired but went back again for fear the Police might come to our camp while we were all away and manure bullock flat with us on our arrival I stopped at the logs and Dan went back to the spring for fear the troopers would come in that way but I soon heard them coming up the creek I told McIntyre to tell them to give up their arms, he spoke to Kennedy who was some distance in front of Scanlon he reached for his revolver and jumped off, on the offside of his horse and got behind a tree when I called on them to throw up their arms and Scanlon who carried the rifle slewed his horse around to gallop away but the horse would not go and as quick as thought he fired at me with the rifle without unslinging it and was in the acting of firing again when I had to shoot him and he fell from his horse.

I could have shot them without speaking but their lives was no good to me. McIntyre jumped on Kennedys horse and I allowed him to go as I did not like to shoot him after he surrendered or I would have shot him as he was between me and Kennedy therefore I could not shoot Kennedy without shooting him first. Kennedy kept firing

from behind the tree my brother Dan advanced and
Kennedy ran I followed him he stopped behind another
tree and fired again. I shot him in the arm pit and he
dropped his revolver and ran I fired again with the gun
as he slewed around to surrender. I did not know he had
dropped his revolver the bullet passed through the right
side of his chest, and he could not live or I would have
let him go had they been my own brothers I could not
help shooting them or else let them shoot me which they
would have done had their bullets been directed as they
intended them. But as for handcuffing Kennedy to a
tree or cutting his ear off or brutally treating any of them
is a falsehood if Kennedy's ear was cut off it was not done
by me and none of my mates was near him after he was
shot I put his cloak over him and left him as well as I
could and were they my own brothers I could not have
been more sorry for them this cannot be called wilful
murder for I was compelled to shoot them or lie down
and let them shoot me it would not be wilful murder if
they packed our remains in, shattered into a mass of
animated gore to Mansfield.

*Glen Tomasetti:*

### STRINGYBARK CREEK

'A sergeant and three constables set out from Mansfield
  town,
At the end of last October for to hunt the Kellys down.
They travelled to the Wombat and thought it quite a lark,
And they camped upon the borders of a creek called
  Stringybark.

They had grub and ammunition there to last them many a
    week,
Next morning two of them rode out to explore all the
    creek,
Leaving McIntyre behind them in the camp to cook the
    grub,
And Lonigan to sweep the floor and boss the washing tub.

Shortly after breakfast Mac thought he heard a noise
And gun in hand he sallied forth to try to find the cause,
He never saw the Kellys planted safe behind a log
And he slithered back to smoke and yarn and wire into the
    grog.

Kelly and his comrades thought they'd take a nearer look
And being short of grub they wished to interview the cook.
And of fire-arms and of cartridges they found they had too
    few,
So they longed to grab the pistols and the ammunition too.

Two bobbies at the stump alone they then were pleased to
    see,
Watching of the billy boiling for the troopers' tea.
They smoked and chatted gaily never thinking of alarms
Till they heard the fearful cry behind: 'Bail up! Throw up
    your arms'.

The traps they started wildly, but Mac he firmly stood,
Threw up his arms while Lonigan made tracks to gain the
    wood,
Reaching round for his revolver but before he touched the
    stock,
Ned Kelly drew his trigger, shot and dropped him like a
    rock.

After searching McIntyre all through the camp then went,
And cleared the guns and cartridges and pistols from the
    tent,
Kelly muttered sadly, as he loaded up his gun,
'O, wasn't it a pity that the bastard tried to run!'

[Collected by Rev. Dr. Percy Jones near Mansfield, Victoria.]

*Ian Jones:* We are sometimes in danger of falling into a one-sided view of the pursuit of the Kelly gang. We tend to forget that the police pursuing the gang were also human beings with problems, were also lonely, also homesick.

I have here some letters written by a most remarkable policeman, Robert Graham, of whom you have probably never heard. His name is worth remembering; and his works are worth remembering. At this time he was a constable who had led a fairly unspectacular career; had been stationed at Camperdown for some little time, by chance, had been the first constable on the scene when the *Loch Ard* was wrecked (and had the distinction, I believe, of washing the seaweed from the hair of Miss Carmichael, one of the two survivors of the wreck). At Camperdown, he had met Mary Kirk, the daughter of a local blacksmith, who was in her teens. Graham himself was then a man of about thirty-four.

He was transferred to Benalla to take part in the pursuit of the Kelly gang, and on St Patrick's day, 1879, he wrote this, the first of several letters to Mary Kirk:

My dear Miss Kirk,

I hope you will forgive me for not carrying out my promise before this but, really, the time I have had to spare would not allow me. I have been away out in the Ranges where the outlaws are supposed to be. It's a very rugged, wild country. I can assure you, I came back here very tired, in fact I was quite knocked up, and had to lie up for a day.

We've not heard anything of the bushrangers since I came up. We're only going out and coming in on a wild goose chase, but we hope to meet with them soon. We have the Queensland blackfellows out now and everyone is looking forward to something being done before long.

I certainly must say that I feel very lonely up here. I have to thank you very much for the wave of the hand-kerchief on the day I left Camperdown. Although I have not written to you, I have by no means forgot to think of you. In fact, you are always uppermost in my mind. I find that the young ladies of this district are very thin and brown, like tanned leather; with the sun.

I had a trip to Beechworth and Wangaratta the other day. Beechworth is a very pretty place. I was wishing in my own mind that you were coming up to see it also.

There are about twenty or thirty constables here at times. As soon as one party comes in, another starts out in their place . . . [*There is an obvious pause. The pen has run out. It is dipped again.*]

It is raining here today. The hills look quite gloomy, like Mount Leura on a wet wintry day. Since I left Camperdown, it seems like a month to me. I enclose a portrait of self to you. Of course, I shall abide by your decision as to its being a good or bad one.

　　With kindest and best wishes to yourself
　　　I remain
　　　　Your sincere friend,
　　　　　Robert Graham.

Other letters followed, in the course of which Constable Graham proposed to Miss Kirk, and was accepted. But there was no hope of his marrying Miss Kirk until the Kelly gang was captured. On 13 September 1879, he ended one of his letters with these sentiments:

If I mistake not this is the month of your birthday. I wish I could get up there so that I could take you a birthday ·present that I am going to give you but I may be able to get away yet. I hope I may, though.

What I should prefer, my dear Mary, is that I should settle in a comfortable nice place and have you along with me. Then I should be happy indeed, and not till then. I am afraid that until these villainous wretches are caught, we will not be able to settle, or if we do we will always be liable to be called away, perhaps for six or eight months from our homes. The same with the married men that is here at the present time. Some of them will have been away from their wives and families so long.

When I have you, my dear, I hope we will not be parted, not for one week, let alone one month.

I must now, my dear, dear, Mary, conclude as I have been called away.

With fond love,
    Your affectionate lover,
        Robert Graham.

There is one last letter. This is dated 24 December 1881. The Kelly Gang has been destroyed. Ned Kelly is dead. Robert Graham has completed more than a year stationed at Greta, home town of the Kellys, in those months after the destruction of the Kelly gang.

He has taken over a farmhouse, refurnished and re-papered it, and is now writing to tell Mary Kirk that at last they can get married and she can come to Greta to live with him as his wife:

My dear,

Do not expect me to write a long letter this time, as my brain is all in a whirl with one thing and another that is to do here with the office, being the end of the year. So many returns have to be made. I only got my permission to get married yesterday evening. How delighted I am, dear, that the affair is coming off at last.

Now too late to wish you a happy Christmas but hope to be with you in person to wish a Happy New Year. I am looking forward with great pleasure to my New Years Gift, to wit, my ever dearest Mary.

With much love and affection,
    I remain, dear
        Your affectionate lover,
            Robert

[Signed with many handsome sweeps and flourishes.]

*Glen Tomasetti:* This is a song of separation. In Ned Kelly's time and well into this century, there was constant separation between lovers, husbands and wives and members of families. Ned and Dan took to the bush, but there were always men leaving home, going shearing or to look for work; leaving the city for the bush, leaving the bush for the city. This song was collected recently by the Victorian Folklore Society. Its style is of the Victorian period and it expresses, very movingly, the feelings of a mother saying goodbye to her son:

'TWAS ON A DAY LIKE THIS

T'was on a day like this, my boy, your brother went away
Not knowing what the future had in store.
Like you my lad, the present was the only time for him
And now our cup of sorrow's brimming o'er.

So you'd better stay at home my lad, until you taller grow
For the miseries of a swagman's life I'm sure you can't
    undergo.
You cannot face the hardships, you'll die of cold I fear,

89

So you'd better stay at home my lad, for your happiest days
   are here.

*Ian Jones:* We often hear in the Kelly legend of Joe Byrne,
poet, letter writer and lover. We have two of Joe's letters
that I know of, both of which, I understand, are now
among the Kelly papers in the State archives.

   The first is a letter dated 26 June 1879, to Joe's lifelong
friend, Aaron Sherritt:

Dear Aaron,
   I write these few stolen lines to let you know I am still
living. I'm not the least afraid of being captured, dear
Aaron. Meet me, you and Jack, this side of Puzzle
Ranges. Neddy and I have come to the conclusion to get
you to join us. I was advised to turn traitor, but I said
I would die at Ned's side first.
   Dear Aaron, it is best for you to join us, Aaron. A short
life and a jolly one. The Lloyds and Quinns want you
shot, but I say no you are on our side. If it is nothing
only the sake of your mother and sisters. We sent that
bloody Hart to your place twice. Did my mother tell
you the message that I left for you. I slept at home three
days on the 24th May. Did Patsy [*Joe's brother Paddy
Byrne, often called Patsy*] give you the booty I left for
you. I intend to pay old Sunday Doig and old Mullane,
O, that bloody snob, where is he? I will make a target
of him. Meet me on next Thursday, you and Jack, and
we will have another bank quite handy. I told Hart to
call last Thursday evening. I would like to know if he
obeyed us or not. If not, we will shoot him.
   If you come on our tracks, close your puss. We know
you were at Kate's several times. You had just gone one
night as we came. We followed you four miles, but returned without success. If you do not meet me where
I ask you, meet me under London you-know. [*London
was London Rock, a large rock in Byrne's Gully behind
the Byrne homestead.*] I will riddle that bloody Mullane

Ned Kelly — a hurried
sketch made at Benalla,
the day after his capture

Kate Kelly. An inaccurate
sketch probably based on
a photograph

The Kelly homestead at Eleven-Mile Creek, Glenrowan West, photographed about 1880. Built in 1877, this is the 'new' homestead where
the Fitzpatrick incident took place. Ned Kelly's half-brother, Jack King,
is standing in front. Although the homestead was still standing in the
1950s, hardly a trace now remains

A grotesque, often-reproduced 'portrait' of Joe Byrne, drawn from a death photo

Steve Hart, about a year before becoming an outlaw. After joining the gang, he grew a light beard

Dan Kelly, about the time he became an outlaw. A portrait by J. Bray of Beechworth

Aaron Sherritt—probably based on a childhood photo. When killed he wore side-burns and a short chin beard

# PROCLAMATION

By His Excellency Sir George Ferguson Bowen, Knight Grand Cross of the Most Distinguished Order of Saint Michael and Saint George, Governor and Commander-in-Chief in and over the Colony of Victoria and its Dependencies, and Vice-Admiral of the same, &c., &c., &c.

WHEREAS under and by virtue of the provisions of "The Felons Apprehension Act 1878," numbered 612, the Governor, with the advice of the Executive Council, is empowered to proclaim the fact that any person has been adjudged and declared to be an outlaw: Now therefore I, the Governor of Victoria, with the advice of the Executive Council, do hereby proclaim that, by a declaration under the hand of His Honor Sir William Foster Stawell, Chief Justice of the Supreme Court of Victoria, dated the fifteenth day of November 1878, and filed of record in the said Supreme Court, **DANIEL KELLY,** of Greta, in the said colony, was adjudged and declared to be an outlaw within the meaning and under the provisions of the said Act.

Given under my hand and the Seal of the Colony, this fifteenth day of November, One thousand eight hundred and seventy-eight, at Melbourne, Victoria, in the forty-second year of Her Majesty's reign.

*Below:* When originally published as a postcard, the three figures in this photograph were incorrectly identified. Detailed examination reveals the three horsemen to be (from left): 'Wild' Wright, scouting for the gang; Ned Kelly riding Joe Byrne's grey 'music' and Steve Hart on his bay. Ned and Steve Hart were described looking exactly as they do here in August, 1879

This prison portrait of Ned Kelly was taken in 1874, when he was 19. Although unflattering, it accurately registers his features—thin mouth, broken nose and 'lazy' left eye

A clumsy fake based on the above prison photo—one at least three versions which are frequently reproduced

*Right:* In many ways, best portrait of Ned. colourful photograph taken to commemorate epic 20-round, bare knu victory over 'Wild' Wr in 1874

*Ned Kelly*
*August 8/1874*
*20 and*
*fought Wild Wright*

Constable Lonigan. A heavily
retouched portrait based on an
equally dubious engraving

Scanlon, killed at Stringyba:
Creck. Ranked as one of th
best bushmen in the Force

Generally claimed to show the finding of Kennedy's body near String
bark Creek, this photograph is almost certainly a reconstruction
Kennedy's body was covered with a waterproof cape—not a blanket, :
here; he was not wearing a hat when found, and would not have wor
the hob-nailed boots seen on the 'dead' man

This 'birds-eye view' gives a reasonably accurate idea of the Glenrowan battle-ground. The buildings are inaccurately drawn, but the positions of Jones' hotel (1), the station (3) and the platelayers' tents (6) are clearly shown

A good reconstruction of Curnow stopping the pilot engine of the police train outside Glenrowan. The train carrying the large force of police can be seen following the pilot engine

A sedate-looking impression of the Last Stand. Ned never in fact reached this position in *front* of the hotel, but more accurately, he wears a yellowish oilskin coat over his armour and tries to shield his wounded left arm behind him

These unique photos were taken by one of several press photographers present at the siege of Glenrowan Inn

*Above:* Smoke begins to rise from the inn after the police have set it alight. Note police taking cover either side of the left-hand tent. (The camp belonged to the railway gang who were forced to break the line.)

*Below:* Ruins of the inn. A sign and water butt remain. At extreme right can be seen paddock sliprails thrown aside by Kelly at the beginning of the siege

Some crude but valuable sketches made at Glenrowan. The guns are
badly proportioned, the armour mostly drawn by guesswork

This study was taken by the photographer Bray at Glenrowan. It shows
the fire-scarred pieces of Dan Kelly's and Steve Hart's armour (two
breastplates, two aprons, two helmets); one of Ned Kelly's shoulder
pieces (between the two helmets), his padded cap and Colt revolving
rifle—both discarded before the Last Stand

Outside Benalla lock-up on 29 June, 1880, Joe Byrne's body is strung up on a door for the photographers. This picture is often claimed to have been taken at Seymour—a memory slip by Julian Ashton

One of five photos taken of Joe's stiffened body as it hung on the lock-up door. He wears tweed trousers, crimean shirt, waistcoat and scarf. A coat hangs in tatters from his left arm. His face and hands are scorched from the fire— Scanlon's ring is still on the little finger of his left hand

A handsome study by Julian Ashton of Ned Kelly in court at Beechworth —Sergeant Steele is standing by the dock. A comparison of this engraving and the photograph of Ned as a boxer, suggests that Julian Ashton used the photo (reversed) as a reference for the work

Redmond Barry—younger and slimmer than he appeared at Ned Kelly's trial

A portrait of Ned taken at his request in the Melbourne Jail the day before his execution. He has tied his flowered neckerchief around the collar of the prison jacket and carefully combed his (by now) long hair

The scene on the gallows—fairly accurately recorded by a newspaper artist. Second from right is Upjohn, the hangman, also in prison garb. The ecclesiastical group includes (probably far left) Dean O'Hea, Ned Kelly's lifelong friend

if I catch him. No more from the enforced outlaw, until
I see yourself.
  I remain
    Yours truly
      You know.


There is another letter written by Joe Byrne, for Aaron
Sherritt, when they were serving a six months' sentence for
being in possession of the hide of a cow 'presumed to have
been stolen'. They went into the prison library one night
and tore out the title page of a book called *Wilson's Tales
of The Borders and Scotland*. This title page was embossed
with the prison library stamp, the broad arrow, and neatly
under this, in pencil, Joe wrote, 'for Jack Sherritt Esq.,
Sheep Station Creek, Reed's Creek near Beechworth'. The
address was neatly written: 'H.M. Gaol, Beechworth'.


Jack,
  I wish you would fetch me a pound of tobacco. You
can send it in easy. Give it to the chap who is working
in the garden, a tall thin chap. I don't ask you to do all
this for nothing. If you secure them two foals and have
them and the blue filly for me when I get out, I will
make you a present of the best . . . I have got [*there is a
passage destroyed by folding which apparently described
where there were a couple of horses hidden.*]
  You must be careful of these few pieces of paper, because it is very hard to get them. This is wrote on the
sly and posted out of the gaol.
  We must now conclude by sending kind love to all.
  We remain your most affectionate brother
    Aaron Sherritt and Joseph Byrne (well known)


Joe had a certain gift for writing doggerel and parodies
— one of which, *The Ballad of Kelly's Gang,* is one of the
best-known Kelly folksongs. This is apparently where he
earned his reputation as the literary brains of the gang.

However, on the basis of his two existing letters, his writing had not quite the stature of the writing in the Jerilderie Letter. I feel that on the basis of this evidence, there is no doubt that Ned Kelly wrote the Jerilderie Letter and not Joe Byrne, as has been suggested from time to time.

*Glen Tomasetti:* People often feel themselves to be not masters but prisoners of their situation. The outlaw has always appealed to the popular imagination, particularly when the majority feels itself unjustly treated. We need heroes, and legend-making does not depend solely on the character of the legendary hero.

In traditional songs as old as those about Robin Hood and as recent as the Kelly ballads, the armed outlaw has certain characteristics. He is often young; he robs the rich and not the poor; he usually kills in self-defence, in defence of friends or of a principle. Revenge may also be an acceptable motive. More indulgence has been granted to the outlaw on horseback than on foot and the romantic view of the eighteenth-century English highwayman travelled to Australia. It was held even by the first Judge Advocate of New South Wales. He wrote that at Christmas 1790 there had been renewed outbreaks of highway robbery around Sydney, but commented, 'at least it is a more manly form of theft than that adopted by the pilfering, dark-loving knaves'.

It seems likely that rejection of the convict past was especially strong in Ned Kelly's lifetime in Victoria, where society took pride in the fact that it had not been founded for the reception of convicts, as had New South Wales and Van Diemen's Land. Kelly's father was a convict and from childhood he may have had a sense of shame, of something to be resented. His adolescent exploits and encounters with the police suggest that he was intelligent and high-spirited and that he had no chance. The 1870s and '80s were hard times for selectors and their children. Old men around Ballarat still tell how their fathers and grandfathers 'never did well'; how they had poor and insufficient land

and were always casual workers. Some moved to the city. Ned Kelly did something much more immediate and dramatic. He rose above his situation by defiance, thereby showing one of the qualities from which legend is made. He became a symbol of rebellion to the death against harsh circumstance.

*The Ballad of Kelly's Gang* was the song written by Joe Byrne. It has almost certainly been rewritten and added to. It is the only ballad which conveys the gay delinquency (also called larrikinism), of the raids on Euroa and Jerilderie. The tune is *The Wearin' of the Green* which was the most popular melody in Victoria for *The Wild Colonial Boy* and was used for many other songs and parodies in the late nineteenth century.

### THE BALLAD OF KELLY'S GANG

Shure Paddy dear, and did ye hear the news that's going round?
On the head of bold Ned Kelly they have placed five thousand pounds,
For Dan, Steve Hart and Joey Byrne, a thousand each they'll give,
But if the sum was double, shure the Kelly boys would live.

'Twas in November '78 the Kelly gang came down,
Just after shooting Kennedy near famous Mansfield Town,
Blood horses rode they all upon, revolvers in their hands,
They took Euroa by surprise and gold was their demand.

Into the bank Ned Kelly walks and 'Bail Up' he did. say,
'Unlock the safe! Hand out your cash! Be quick and don't delay!

Your wives and children too must come, so make them
    look alive.
Step into these conveyances, we'll take you for a drive.'

They drove them to a station about five miles away,
Where twenty men already had been bailed up all the day,
A hawker also shared their fate as everybody knows,
He came in handy to the gang, supplying them with clothes.

They rode into Jerilderie Town at twelve o'clock at night,
They roused the troopers in their beds all in a dreadful
    fright,
They took them in their nightshirts, ashamed am I to tell,
They covered them with revolvers and they locked them in
    a cell.

Next day being Sunday, of course they must be good,
They dressed themselves in troopers' clothes and Neddy
    chopped the wood.
Nobody there suspected them, for troopers all they pass,
And Dan, the most religious, took the sergeant's wife to
    mass.

Monday morning early, still masters of the ground,
They took their horses to the forge and had them shod all
    round,
Back they brought and mounted them, they plan the raid
    so well,
In company with the troopers they stuck up the Royal
    Hotel.

They shouted freely for all hands and paid for all they
    drank,
Then two of them remained in charge and two went to the
    bank,
They bailed up all the bankers' clerks and robbed them of
    their gold,
They caught the manager in his bath, all blue with funk
    and cold.

They destroyed communication by telegraph at last,
Of robberies and plunderings they had a perfect feast,

Where they have gone's a mystery, the police they cannot
  tell,
So until we hear from them again, I'll bid yers all farewell.

*Ian Jones:* We have heard in this ballad about Euroa and
Jerilderie. It was written before the Glenrowan hold-up
was even dreamed of. We have heard a lot about Glenrowan already with its legendary Last Stand of Ned Kelly.

This episode has been much misrepresented, much misunderstood. Here is an account given by Sergeant Steele.
It was written some years after Glenrowan, but compares
in detail very well with his earlier accounts. Here he includes a few details which he has obviously recalled in
tranquillity, things which he forgot in the heat of the
moment when he gave the first descriptions of that unique
dawn battle.

Steele arrives at Glenrowan in the very early hours of
the Monday morning when it was still dark and is crouched
in the bush only a matter of some ten yards from the rear
door of the hotel. He has fired at and seriously wounded
a civilian. Now it is approaching dawn. Stiff and numb
with cold, with his double-barrelled shotgun and his tweed
hat and tweed jacket, Steele crouches, staring through the
mist towards the low grey shape of the Glenrowan Inn.

Sometime after daybreak and before the sun appeared,
I heard some disturbance behind me, and in the dim
light I could see the figure of a man approaching. I heard
someone call to him: 'Don't come down here, you fool,
you'll be shot'. but he came walking quietly along. Then
a constable cried out: 'Look out. It's one of the beggars
and he's covered with iron', and there were several shots
at once fired at him.

He was then 150 yards or so from me, and, in the dull
light, I was first convinced that the man was Tommy
Reid, a well-known district blackfellow. The figure was
exactly like his at the distance and in the half light. A
tall man, with a blanket around his shoulders, and thin

black legs. I called out, therefore, to men in my direction to be careful of the shooting. But the deception became apparent when the outlaw (for it was Ned Kelly) came closer, and what I thought was the blackfellow's blanket was a fawn coloured waterproof cape or cloak and black strapping on a pair of grey trousers had given the appearance of thin black legs.

He was not far from me, about 50 or 60 yards away, when he threw the cloak off him and began firing a revolver at several police who were closer to him. They ran for shelter and fired a number of shots at him and I could plainly hear the bullets strike his armour. All this time he kept gradually approaching the hotel, moving to the side from time to time to fire at constables sheltering behind a tree. He was practically clearing a passage, as none stood his ground, but ran from tree to tree. He discharged three revolvers and it seemed to me that he was thus engaged for fifteen or twenty minutes. That is, from the time he made his first appearance out of the bush behind us.

Kelly then leisurely sat down between three trees standing close together, and I could see that he was reloading his revolvers. Some police were quite close to him, and I called out to rush him, as his revolvers were empty. But no-one made the attempt. I then thought of doing it myself, but first looked from behind a tree at the back door of the hotel. Immediately two shots were fired, but I determined to take the risk and made a run towards Kelly. He stood up at once and, resting a revolver against a tree, fired two shots at me. At the same time, a bullet fired from the hotel hit the ground alongside my feet. I threw myself down and this probably saved me, and it deceived Kelly for the time. He thought that I was injured, but the only inconvenience that I had so far suffered was from a quantity of sand that had got into my eye when I fell, and caused me such pain at the moment that I had to rub the eye violently and this motion might have misled the outlaw.

Just at this time, a number of civilians ran from near the hotel to the railway station and Kelly walked away from the trees and, tapping his apron and helmet with a revolver, called out: 'Come on boys, we'll whip the lot of the beggars'. He then levelled and fired at the running figures. Seeing his attention diverted, I stood up and rushed at him.

We were fourteen or fifteen yards apart. By some peculiarity of fate, his mare trotted between us before I had reached him and I had my gun levelled, before he had time to take action. Notwithstanding that, he turned with some smartness. As he was levelling his revolver at me, I fired at his leg, which I saw was not protected by armour, and he staggered back. As he staggered, he spread his legs apart to save himself from falling, and while he did so, he exposed the opening in the armour on his hip. I fired a second shot at the spot. My gun was loaded with buck-shot.

He then sank down, his helmet falling off and partly supporting his head. I rushed to seize him, and, as I stooped, he raised his arm and pointed the revolver backwards at me, but the shot was discharged into the air as I grabbed his wrist. The bullet cut the rim of my hat and my face was slightly blackened by smoke. I at once wrenched the revolver from his hand.

Steele then described how Kelly was disarmed, thrown to the ground and stripped of his armour. He then comments:

As indicative of Ned Kelly's pluck, I may add that, when I was travelling from Melbourne with him when he was being brought to stand his preliminary trial, he told me that he was hidden in the bush when I and my party arrived from Wangaratta on the morning of the capture. As I passed within a yard or two of him, he could have shot me in the back. He repeated a remark that I remember making to the constable of whom I was in charge, and in other ways convinced me of the truth of his statement.

The facts show that he was considerably outside the cordon of police on that fateful morning, and could easily have escaped had he so desired. When I saw him walking towards the hotel, he came from the direction of the spot he indicated. A circumstance in his subsequent action convinced me of the truth of his statement, that he had returned in an endeavour to save his companions and first thought to drive the police away from the side and rear of the hotel.

*Ian Jones:* Ned Kelly was captured. The gang was destroyed. The Glenrowan pub was burnt to the ground. Ned Kelly was taken to Benalla and spent the night in a cell next to which lay the stiffened body of his best friend Joe Byrne.

Ned was put on a train the next morning, sent to Melbourne, nursed back to health, brought up to Beechworth for the preliminary trial, taken back to Melbourne for his trial proper, tried and found guilty, and sentenced to death.

At the end of the trial occurred, between Ned Kelly and Mr Justice Barry, one of the most remarkable exchanges in legal history. I cannot agree with Professor Manning Clark that Kelly's spirit was changed. To me this is still the defiant outlaw, standing up to the last against the people who had surrounded him and destroyed him.

After the sentence, Ned Kelly dictated a whole series of statements to David Gaunson, hoping that they would be published. None of them appeared during the remaining days of Kelly's life. But one of them has come down to us, dictated in his cell in the Melbourne Jail only a matter of days before his death.

I don't pretend that I have lived a blameless life, or that one fault justifies another. But the public judging a case like mine should remember that the darkest life may have a bright side. After the worst has been said against a man, he may, if he's heard, tell a story in his own rough way that will lead them to soften their harshest thoughts against him and find as many excuses for him as he would plead for himself.

For my own part, I don't care one straw about my life nor the result of the trial, and I know very well from the stories I've been told how I am spoken of; that the public at large execrate my name. The newspapers have not spoken of me with that patient tolerance generally extended to men awaiting trial and are assumed according to the boast of British Justice to be innocent until they are proved to be guilty. But I don't mind, for I am the last that curries public favour or dreads the public frown. Let the hand of the law strike me down if it will, but I ask that my story may be heard and considered, not that I wish to avert any decree the law may deem necessary to vindicate justice or win a word of pity from anyone.

If my lips teach the public that men are made mad by bad treatment, and if the police are taught that they may exasperate to madness men they persecute and ill-treat, my life will not be entirely thrown away. People who live in large towns have no idea of the tyrannical conduct of police far removed from court. They have no idea of the harsh over-bearing manner in which they execute their duties, of how they neglect their duties and abuse their powers.

Edward Kelly

Efforts to gain the reprieve of Edward Kelly failed and, on the night of 10 November 1880, he prepared to face his execution at ten o'clock the following morning.

Ned Kelly had his last meal — roast lamb, green peas, and a bottle of claret. He had a last interview with his mother, who spoke those famous words: 'Mind you die like a Kelly, son, as bravely as you lived.' He had his last interview with Kate Kelly, with Margaret Skillion, with his cousins Tom and Kate Lloyd. He was then left in the cell, closely watched by the warders who kept guard all night to make sure that he did not commit suicide before he could be executed. As the night wore on, Ned Kelly started to sing. At first he sang some of the ballads. He probably sang *The Ballad of Kelly's Gang* written by Joe. Then, after a while he began to sing more sentimental songs, old bush ballads that he had sung in younger and happier days.

*Glen Tomasetti:*

### THE DYING STOCKMAN

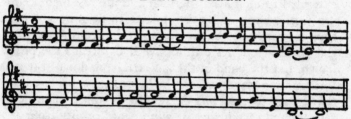

A strapping young stockman lay dying,
His saddle supporting his head;
His two mates around him were crying
As he rose on his pillow and said:

   Chorus:

Wrap me up in my stockwhip and blanket
And bury me deep down below,
Where the dingoes and crows can't molest me,
In the shade where the coolibahs grow.

Cut down a couple of saplings,
Place one at my head and my toe;
Carve on them crossed stockwhip and saddle
To show there's a stockman below.

   Chorus:

Oh had I the flight of a bronze wing
High on my pinions I'd fly
Back to the land of my childhood,
And there I would lay down and die.

Chorus:

There's tea in the battered old billy,
Place the pannikins out in a row

Let's drink to the next merry meeting,
In the place where all good stockmen go.
    Chorus:

*Ian Jones:* Eventually, on this last night of his life, Ned
Kelly stopped singing. The story is taken up by a reporter
who coldly and objectively looks at the last eight hours of
Ned Kelly's life.

He retired to rest at last, about half past one o'clock
this morning, but was very uneasy and restless until about
half past two o'clock when he fell asleep. He slept quietly
until five o'clock this morning. He then rose and occupied about twenty minutes in his devotions.

After this the convict appeared tolerably contented
and calm, for he went so far as to indulge in a little
vocalization. Although the songs which he sang were not
sacred, they were of the better class of secular composi-
tion, and contained nothing in themselves offensive.

During the time between half past five o'clock and
nine o'clock, Kelly occasionally lay down and rested
for a while. At nine o'clock the Very Reverend Dean
Donaghy, the Chaplain of the Gaol, who had been in
constant attendance on the condemned man, arrived to
administer the last rites of the Church and to be present
with him in his last moments. The Very Reverend Dean
was, of course, left alone with the condemned man and
equally, of course, what passed between them will never
be revealed.

At about half past nine o'clock, the Very Reverend
Dean O'Hea of Coburg, who knew Kelly in his boyhood,
and is even said to have baptised him and was therefore
anxious to comfort him as far as possible in his last
moments, arrived, and was at once conducted to the condemned cell where he remained with Dean Donaghy and
the culprit until a tap at the door announced the arrival
of the Sherriff.

Colonel Rede the Sherriff of the Central Bailiwick,

NED KELLY: MAN AND MYTH

was attended by Mr Ellis, the under-Sherriff, and presented himself at the door of the condemned cell punctually at ten o'clock to demand the body of Edward Kelly in order to carry out the awful sentence of death.

Mr Castieau, the Governor of the Gaol, had some little time previously visited the prisoner and seen his irons knocked off and, the necessary warrant being presented by the Sherriff, he tapped at the door and the prisoner was made acquainted of the fearful fact that his last hour had arrived.

All this time, Upjohn, the hangman, who for the first time officiated in this horrible capacity, so far as is known in this colony, had been unseen. But, upon the door of the cell being opened, the signal was given and he emerged from the condemned cell opposite that occupied by his first victim. He stepped across to the scaffold quietly and, as he did so, quietly turned his head and looked down upon the spectators, revealing a fearfully repulsive countenance.

Upjohn disappeared into the condemned cell and proceeded to pinion Kelly with a broad and strong leather strap. The prisoner remarked: 'You needn't pinion me', but was, of course, told that it was indispensible, and the hangman rapidly performed this portion of his task.

Preceded by the crucifix which was held before him by the officiating priest, Kelly was then led onto the platform. He had not been shaved or cropped and was in prison clothes. He seemed calm and collected but paler than usual. This effect might have been produced by the white night cap placed over his head but not drawn over his face. As he stepped on the drop, he remarked in a low tone: 'Such is life'.

The hangman then proceeded to adjust the rope, the Dean in the meantime reading the prayer proper to the Catholic Church on such occasion. The prisoner winced slightly at the first touch of the rope but quickly recovered himself and moved his head in order to facilitate the work of Upjohn in fixing the knot properly.

No sooner was the rope fixed than, without the prisoner being afforded the chance of saying anything more, the signal was given and the hangman, pulling down the catch, stepped back and, withdrawing the bolt, had done his work. At the same instant, the mortal remains of Edward Kelly were swinging some eight feet below where they had previously been standing.

At first it appeared that his death had been instantaneous for there was for a second or two only the usual shudder which passes through the frame of hanged men. But then the legs were drawn up for some distance and fell suddenly again. This movement was repeated several times. But finally all motion ceased, and, at the end of four minutes, all was over and Edward Kelly had gone to a higher tribunal to answer for his faults and crimes.

The body was allowed to remain hanging for the usual time and the formal inquest was afterwards held when the remains were buried within the precincts of the Gaol. An application by the relatives for the body was refused.

This is the last melancholy act in the history of the Kelly Gang led by Edward Kelly, during the career of which so many many lives had been sacrificed.

# CHARGE FOR AN INDICTABLE OFFENCE.

THE information and complaint of *Thomas McIntyre* of *Melbourne* in the Colony of Victoria, *Constable* taken this *thirtieth* day of *July* in the year of our Lord One thousand eight hundred and *eighty*, before the undersigned, *One* of Her Majesty's Justices of the Peace in and for the said *Bailiwick* who saith that*

*Edward Kelly on the twenty sixth day of October in the year one thousand eight hundred and seventy eight at Stringy Bark Creek in the Northern Bailiwick feloniously wilfully and of his malice aforethought did kill and murder one Thomas Lonigan*

*Thomas McIntyre*

Sworn before *me* the day and year first above-mentioned, at *Melbourne* in the said Colony.

*Thomas Mohns* J.P.

# 5

# *Regina v. Edward Kelly*

## PROFESSOR LOUIS WALLER

*Louis Waller has been Sir Leo Cussen Professor of Law at Monash University since 1965. A graduate of Melbourne and Oxford universities, he was Bicentennial Fellow in Criminal Law at the University of Pennsylvania in 1964, visiting Professor at the University of Kent in 1971 and a consultant for the Canadian Law Reform Commission in 1974-5.*

### INTRODUCTION

The criminal trial is an occasion of great drama. I think that in 1880 a criminal trial was perhaps *the* dramatic public occasion in any community. In our community today the great public dramatic event is the League football match, but the criminal trial still retains its own peculiar fascination. This may be because it represents the public repudiation of wrong and the vindication of right. On a less lofty plane, it may be because for many of us there is truth in the view expressed by Sir James Stephen with his usual force more than a hundred years ago: 'The criminal law stands to the passion of revenge in much the same relation as marriage to the sexual appetite.'[1]

We want to see revenge taken — respectably.

Of all criminal trials those for capital offences are the most dramatic, the most carefully considered, the most closely observed. In October 1880 Edward Kelly was not just a man standing his trial for the capital offence of murder. He was also a man who had been put outside the

[1] *A General View of the Criminal Law* (1863), p. 99.

105

law, labelled 'outlaw', by a legal process which had never been imported into Australia as part of the common law heritage, and which had to be introduced by special legislation enacted in great haste in 1878. It is not strange then to find that public interest in his trial was deep and persistent. The interest has persisted beyond that decade and beyond that century.

My purpose today is to look at this last encounter which Ned Kelly had with law and order in Victoria. I propose to describe the trial, and to comment on it, but in addition I propose to examine Kelly's defence of his trial in some detail.

### THE PRELIMINARY EXAMINATION

After Kelly was captured at Glenrowan on 29 June 1880, he was treated for his various wounds and kept in custody pending a preliminary examination by a magistrate or justice into the accusations that Kelly had murdered Constables Lonigan and Scanlon. The accusations of murder were made by Constable McIntyre, who swore an information in respect of the murder of Lonigan as follows:

> The information and complaint of Thomas McIntyre of Melbourne in the Colony of Victoria, Constable taken this 30th day of July, in the year of our Lord One thousand eight hundred and eighty before the undersigned, one of Her Majesty's Justices of the Peace in and for the said Bailiwick [Central Bailiwick, Melbourne] who saith that Ned Kelly on the 26th day of October in the year One thousand eight hundred and seventy eight at Stringybark Creek in the Northern Bailiwick feloniously wilfully and with malice aforethought did kill and murder one Thomas Lonigan.

The preliminary examination into the informations was conducted in the Court of Petty Sessions at Beechworth

106

before Mr W. H. Foster, a police magistrate. David Gaunson, a Melbourne solicitor and member of the Legislative Assembly, appeared for Kelly. Kelly was committed to stand his trial at Beechworth in October.

## CRIMINAL JUSTICE IN VICTORIA IN 1880

The administration of criminal justice in Victoria in 1880 did not differ in many respects from the administration of that part of the law today. The preliminary examination was held before justices or a magistrate sitting at a place convenient to the scene of the alleged crime. The accused was committed to stand his trial before a superior court which would sit in the district. The testimony of the witnesses called by the Crown at the preliminary hearing was taken down in writing and signed by the witnesses. These depositions formed the basis of the Crown's case at the trial and also served to give the defence notice of the case which it would have to meet.

In 1874 the administration of criminal justice in Victoria was specifically affected by the creation of a separate system of criminal courts. Victoria was already divided into bailiwicks, or distinct districts, and for each bailiwick there was established a Court of Assize. In the Central Bailiwick, which was in fact the Melbourne metropolitan area, the new criminal court was denominated the 'Central Criminal Court'. Judges of the Supreme Court of Victoria were appointed as judges to preside in the Central Criminal Court and in the Courts of Assize. Kelly was committed to stand his trial in the Court of Assize sitting at Beechworth, which was one of the assize towns for the Northern Bailiwick. This system of courts did not long survive in Victoria; it was abolished by the *Judicature Act* 1883 which revested the criminal jurisdiction exercised by the Courts of Assize and the Central Criminal Court in the Supreme Court itself, where it remains today.

Shortly after Kelly was committed for trial, the Crown applied for a change of venue, contending that it would be gravely prejudiced if Kelly was tried in Beechworth.[2] The application succeeded and the venue was shifted to Melbourne. It was in Melbourne between 15 and 30 October 1880 that the legal proceedings which culminated in Kelly's conviction for the murder of Constable Lonigan took place.

If all of us had been able to be present in the Central Criminal Court in Russell Street during that month we would not have felt that we had intruded on legal proceedings which were strange and archaic. We would have found that the lawyers looked much the same as lawyers engaged in similar proceedings today. Counsel wore the already traditional black robes, white bands and horsehair wig. The judge sitting in the Central Criminal Court wore robes of red. The court crier wore much the same kind of high-buttoned coat which some Melbourne court officials still wear today. Etchings and drawings of the day confirm these statements, and reveal a courtroom, with bench, jury-box, and dock, very like some of the rooms in the Law Courts in William Street.

We would also have found that, by and large, the criminal process was itself the same as it is today. Kelly was tried according to procedures which were well established, and which in many regards are little changed today. There were, however, some substantial differences which I want to point out, because they assume significance later.

In 1880, a man standing his trial for a felony like murder, was not competent to give sworn evidence in his own behalf. His mouth was closed, as Kelly's counsel was to say in his speech to the jury. It seems curious to us today that this should be so, and the reasons advanced to support that incompetency do not really bear modern examination. One was that a man who had such a deep interest in the outcome of the case must be regarded as an untrustworthy witness.

[2] The application was made in reliance upon section 330 of the *Criminal Law and Practice Statute, 1864*; see now section 359 of the *Crimes Act 1958*. The change may be made 'for good cause shown'. For the procedure then applicable see H. Gurner, *The Practice of the Criminal Law of the Colony of Victoria* (1871), p. 59.

The general rule of the common law was that all interested persons were incompetent and it seemed to apply particularly to men accused of crimes.

The other reason was a perverted extension of the rule, well established in the common law, that a man was not to be compelled to condemn himself out of his own mouth — the privilege against self-incrimination. It was thought that if the accused went into the witness box to give sworn evidence, he might be made to inculpate himself, and this would be grave erosion of this privilege, and a revival of the practices associated with the courts in bygone days, especially the Star Chamber.[3] It was not until 1891 that this embargo was lifted in Victoria, and persons accused of crimes were permitted, if *they* so desired, to give sworn evidence in their own defence. It was a further seven years before this important amelioration became part of the law of England. Today we accept it as a matter of course and now counsel's boot is very much on the other foot. Instead of counsel for the defendant being able to say to the jury, 'My client's mouth is sealed', in some jurisdictions (not in Victoria), it is counsel for the Crown who may comment, 'The accused is allowed to go to the witness box and tell his story on oath and face cross-examination. Is it not curious that he has not done so?'[4]

The accused person was permitted to make an unsworn statement from the dock which might be taken into account by the jury when it came to decide whether or not he was innocent or guilty. Sir Redmond Barry was to remind the jury that Kelly had not taken the opportunity to tell his unsworn story from the dock. The right to make such a statement is still preserved in Victoria.[5]

There is a second important difference. In 1880 there existed no general appellate process in criminal cases,

[3] *Cross on Evidence* (3rd ed., 1967), pp. 140, 145.
[4] See *Crimes Act* 1958, section 399; the judge may comment on the accused's failure to testify if he makes an unsworn statement. In England he may comment on his failure even if he remains altogether silent. See *Criminal Evidence Act,* 1898, section 1, proviso (b).
[5] See *Crimes Act* 1958, section 399, proviso (g).

whereby a man convicted before a judge and jury could challenge his conviction before a Court of Criminal Appeal on the grounds, say, that evidence which ought not to have been admitted was admitted, or that the trial judge had made mistakes in summing up the law to the jury, or that there had been some other miscarriage of justice at his trial. The processes of review available were meagre. If a serious mistake occurred in certain procedures during the trial — if an unqualified juror was sworn to the jury, or if there was some other kind of interference with the jury — then the accused man after his conviction could apply to the Supreme Court for what is called a *venire de novo,* and if his application succeeded a new trial was ordered. The basis for such a ruling is that the trial is a complete nullity.[6] In addition the accused, through his counsel, could ask the trial judge at the end of the whole case to reserve a question or questions of law for Full Court, stating in writing what the difficulty was and leaving the verdict dependent on the Full Court's ruling. It lay within the trial judge's discretion whether or not to grant such an application. This procedure, commonly called 'Crown Cases Reserved,' permitted the Full Court of three judges to determine uncertain or difficult questions of law arising in a criminal prosecution and in the light of the determination to dispose of the case finally or, in Victoria, to order a new trial.[7]

In England the dreadful errors which occurred in the case of Adolf Beck ultimately led to the establishment of a separate Court of Criminal Appeal in 1907. That Court was established specifically to hear appeals by convicted persons on grounds of appeal which involved 'questions of

[6] See Gurner, *op. cit.,* p. 173. Notice that a distinction is drawn on p. 174 in respect of misdemeanours, where Gurner takes the view that there was, in England, more ample powers in the superior courts to review decisions of inferior tribunals (like Courts of Quarter Sessions) and to order new trials where the presiding judge had erred.
[7] *Criminal Law and Practice Statute* 1864, sections 389 and 390; see Gurner, *op cit.,* pp. 177-82. This procedure is still preserved in Victoria to permit a judge to state a case for consideration by the Full Court when any difficulty in point of law arises; see *Crimes Act* 1958, sections 446-50.

fact alone, or questions of mixed law and fact, or any other ground which appears to be . . . a sufficient ground of appeal'. The English legislation was copied almost exactly in Victoria in 1914 and the Full Court of the Supreme Court of Victoria was invested with the powers which had been conferred in England on the newly established Court of Criminal Appeal.[8]

Finally, there is the rule about the burden of proof. We are all accustomed today, from our reading and from our own observations of criminal trials, and from watching dramatic portrayals on television and in the cinema, to hearing the trial judge, when he comes to charge the jury, state, usually several times, that the burden of proof lies upon the Crown. It will be said that it is necessary for the Crown to satisfy the jury, in the famous formula, 'beyond any reasonable doubt' on each issue which has been raised during the course of the trial. There is a considerable body of legal opinion which holds the view that, in prosecutions for murder, this has been the law only since 1935, when the House of Lords decided the now famous case of *Woolmington* v. *Director of Public Prosecutions*. In that case Viscount Sankey L.C. said:

Throughout the web of the English Criminal Law one golden thread is always to be seen, that it is the duty of the prosecution to prove the prisoner's guilt subject to that I have already said as to the defence of insanity and subject also to any statutory exception. If, at the end of and on the whole of the case, there is a reasonable doubt, created by the evidence given by either the prosecution or the prisoner, as to whether the prisoner killed the deceased with malicious intention, the prosecution has not made out the case and the prisoner is entitled to an acquittal. No matter what the charge or where the trial,

[8] See *Criminal Appeal Act* 1914. See now Part VI of the *Crimes Act* 1958. In England the Court of Criminal Appeal was abolished in 1966 and its powers are today exercised by the Court of Appeal, which has Criminal and Civil Divisions.

the principle that the prosecution must prove the guilt of the prisoner is part of the common law of England and no attempt to whittle it down can be entertained. When dealing with a murder case the Crown must prove (a) death as the result of a voluntary act of the accused and (b) malice of the accused.[8a]

Shortly after this speech was made Sir Owen Dixon[9] delivered a paper at the first Convention of the Law Council of Australia in which he showed that the judgement in *Woolmington's case* represented a new, though wholly to be welcomed, development. In his view, the law had been as Sir Michael Foster put it:

'. . . The fact of killing being first proved, all the circumstances of accident, necessity, or infirmity are to be satisfactorily proved by the prisoner, unless they arise out of the evidence produced against him; for the law presumeth the fact to have been founded in malice, until the contrary appeareth.'[10]

In 1880 it would therefore have been entirely appropriate for the trial judge to tell the jury that it was the defendant who bore the burden of proving that he was acting in self-defence or under duress, or whatever other excuse or justification, and who ran the risk of conviction if he failed. In his charge to the jury, as reproduced in the *Age* of 30 October 1880, Sir Redmond Barry does not refer specifically to the burden of proof at all. He said (and his words are reported in *oratio obliqua*): 'Malice was twofold. It might be proved by expression made use of by the prisoner, which showed a malevolent disposition, and that he had an intention to take away the life of another man without lawful cause.'

He did not use any of the now traditional expressions, according to these reports, to warn the jury that they must

[8a] [1935] A. C., 462, at 481.
[9] *The Development of the Law of Homicide,* and reprinted in *Jesting Pilate* (Law Book Co., 1965), p. 61.
[10] *A Discourse on Homicide* (Crown Law. 3rd ed., 1809).

be satisfied by the prosecution of every element of the offence beyond any reasonable doubt. He may have so charged them, and the reporters may have omitted these expressions as too commonplace. But in the light of what has been said before it is unlikely that Sir Redmond Barry departed from the then clearly accepted judicial understanding of the burden of proof in a prosecution for murder.

## THE TRIAL

I come now to the trial itself, to those two weeks between 15 and 29 October 1880. The judge presiding in the Central Criminal Court was His Honour Mr Justice Sir Redmond Barry, KCMG, and his Associate Mr John G. F. Horne. By a coincidence this judge had presided over the earlier trial of people intimately connected with Kelly, who were charged as aiders and abettors in the wounding of Constable Fitzpatrick; one of the prisoners then convicted was Kelly's mother.

Kelly's defence was undertaken by David Gaunson, who had acted for him at the preliminary examination. The Crown had agreed to pay for Kelly's defence, since apparently he had no funds. The fruits of Euroa and Jerilderie were no more. On 15 October an application was made on Kelly's behalf to Sir Redmond Barry, presiding in the Central Criminal Court, seeking a postponement of the trial to the November sittings. The application was opposed by the Crown, which stated that Kelly's solicitor had known the proposed date of trial since 25 August and had had the depositions on 8 August. It was refused.

On 18 October Kelly was presented on two charges of murder, in respect of Constables Lonigan and Scanlon. He was arraigned and he pleaded 'not guilty'. The presiding judge was still Sir Redmond Barry. The Prosecutor for the Queen was Charles Alexander Smyth; Arthur Wolfe Chomley, Prosecutor for the Queen at the Beechworth Court of Assize, appeared with him. Henry Massy Bindon, barrister-at-law, appeared for Kelly. Bindon at once applied to have the trial postponed until the next sittings. The point of the application was that Gaunson, Kelly's attorney, was seeking further funds from the Crown so he could brief experienced counsel in the person of Hickman Molesworth, a barrister-at-law of sixteen years' standing, in whose name Bindon made the application. Bindon himself had been at the Victorian Bar for less than ten months. This application was again opposed by Smyth, who pointed out that the Crown had advanced funds on the usual terms: 7 guineas for attorney, 7 guineas for counsel, and 5 shillings for his clerk's fee. An application for more funds, he went on, would be favourably entertained if the length of the trial warranted it. But at the end of his argument Smyth gracefully said he was 'loth to do anything which would convey an impression that the prisoner had been improperly treated' and suggested an adjournment for one week. Sir Redmond Barry said he would not be disengaged until 28 October, and the trial was accordingly adjourned until that day.

When it resumed, Bindon asked for a further adjournment, stating that it had proved impossible for Gaunson to brief Molesworth and that he had therefore been asked at three days' notice to undertake the defence. He wanted more time to prepare. The application was brusquely refused, a jury was empanelled and Kelly given in their charge, and the trial proper began. It was a trial of the first charge, be it noted, the murder of Thomas Lonigan.

Smyth began in the traditional way. He opened his case, outlining the facts which the witnesses he was to call would prove. Then without further ado he began to call his evidence.

On the first day, eight witnesses were called for the Crown. Detective Michael Edward Ward, of whom we have heard something already, was first. Then came Constable Patrick Day, stationed at Benalla, and then the most important witness of all, Constable Thomas McIntyre.

114

Ward and Day were called to produce, from official custody, warrants issued in respect of Edward Kelly. Ward produced the horse-stealing warrant — the warrant that had been the cause of Constable Fitzpatrick's going off on what was the first ill-fated expedition in the Kelly outbreak. Day produced the warrant charging Kelly with wounding Constable Fitzpatrick with intent to murder him, identified as the reason which sent the police party into the Wombat Ranges. Constable McIntyre, the stage having been set, was called to tell *oyant et voyant* — of his own hearing and sight — the story of what happened when Lonigan was killed.

It may be a surprise to learn that, after McIntyre, there was still a long parade of Crown witnesses. On that first day, as well as the three men that I have mentioned, there were called George Stephens, a groom at Younghusband's station near Euroa; William Fitzgerald, who was also employed there, as a labourer, when the Kellys robbed the bank at Euroa; Henry Dudley and Robert McDougall, who had both blundered into Younghusband's station as members of a shooting party (and who were both employed in the Government printing office in Melbourne); James Gloster, who hawked drapery and such-like through north-eastern Victoria, and who was visiting Younghusband's. Gloster and all the witnesses after McIntyre were called to repeat admissions which Kelly was said to have made at various times to them about the shooting at Stringybark Creek.

The first day's proceedings adjourned at 6.02 in the afternoon, with an announcement by Sir Redmond Barry that he would be prepared to sit very late the next day should it be necessary. He was unwilling, he said, to have the jury confined (as was necessary once the trial had started and the prisoner had been given into their charge) while the racing week was on in Melbourne.

The second day of trial began at 9 a.m. on 29 October. The Crown continued to call its witnesses. Frank Beacroft, Gloster's assistant; Robert Scott, the manager of the

National Bank at Euroa; Constable Henry Richards of the N.S.W. police, stationed at Jerilderie; Edward Living, the accountant at the Bank of N.S.W. in Jerilderie; John Tarleton, manager at that bank when the Kellys held it up in 1879; Senior Constable John Kelly of the Victoria police; and Sergeant Arthur Steele, of the Victoria police, were called in that order. Again, all were called to give evidence of admissions which Kelly was said to have made to them at various times about what happened at Stringybark Creek in October 1878. Kelly and Steele gave evidence of conversations after Kelly was captured at Glenrowan. The last witness for the Crown was Dr Samuel Reynolds. He testified that he had examined the body of Lonigan, from which examination he had inferred that the body had been struck by four bullets; he gave the formal evidence that Lonigan had died from gunshot wounds. His evidence proved that the man Kelly was charged with murdering was indeed dead, and was indeed Thomas Lonigan.

Sixteen witnesses in all gave the Queen's evidence; two to set the stage, one to tell the story, and the rest, except for Dr Reynolds, to put before the Court, out of Kelly's own mouth, a confession in the round, that he had 'feloniously, wilfully and with malice aforethought killed and murdered Thomas Lonigan, a Constable of Police'. For, curiously, though Kelly could not give sworn evidence, his confessions or admissions were admissible against him as statements against his interest. This is the most important exception, long recognized, to the rule against hearsay.

As soon as the Crown's case ended, Bindon, who had not been completely silent during its course but who had cross-examined a number of the witnesses, asked the trial judge to note his objection to the admission in evidence of what had occurred after Lonigan had been killed. 'He contended as the prisoner was not being tried for the murder of Kennedy or Scanlon, that therefore no evidence should have been given in regard to them' (The *Age*, 30 October 1880). His argument must have been that this evidence was inadmissible, as relevant only to show a generally evil disposition, and was grossly prejudicial.[11] It went to show, not that he killed Constable Lonigan (Bindon said or ought to have said), but that he was a man who engaged in other unlawful activities, a 'dog with a bad name'. Bindon asked the judge to reserve a special case for the Full Court, so that they could pass on his objection. Sir Redmond Barry refused. He held the evidence was properly admitted, firstly, because it was an integral part of the events of that day at Stringybark Creek — it was part of what lawyers called the *res gestae,* the things done; and secondly, it was admissible in order to show the *motive,* by which Barry must have meant the state of mind, which Kelly had, 'to show whether the shooting of Constable Lonigan were accidental or justifiable' (The *Age,* 30 October 1880). As to the first ground of admissibility, I consider that Sir Redmond Barry was wrong. The evidence of what happened when Lonigan was shot was self-contained, and could be understood without any reference whatsoever to what came after. The *res gestae* rules, though permitting the reception of much that seems otherwise inadmissible as hearsay or opinion, only permit this reception if the tribunal cannot understand what happens before unless it knows what came immediately afterwards.[12] As far as the second ground is concerned, Barry was right in admitting the evidence as going not just to Kelly's disposition to violence, but to his particular state of mind and his beliefs when he shot Lonigan.[13] This should be remembered when Kelly's defence is considered.

The Court was then adjourned for an hour so that Bindon could consider what course he was going to take. On resumption it was announced that no evidence would be called on Kelly's behalf, and that he would rely for his whole defence on what Bindon had managed to do for

[11] See *Makin* v. *Attorney-General of New South Wales* [1894] A.C. 51.

[12] See *Cross on Evidence* (3rd ed., 1967). The final form of the rule is still unsettled, and it may have been widely regarded by Sir Redmond Barry.

[13] See, e.g., *Makin's case,* n. 11 *supra,* for an illustration of admissibility.

him in his cross-examination of the Crown witnesses and on Bindon's concluding address to the jury. According to the practice already established (to which we still adhere today) since the accused was calling no evidence, his counsel had the famous last word, the opportunity to address the jury after the Crown Prosecutor addressed them. Smyth spoke to the jury at some length and took particular occasion to point out 'the cowardly nature', as he put it, of the attack made by Kelly. He portrayed Kelly as a poltroon who never engaged the forces of law and order in combat unless he was in a position of complete supremacy. He also said that, even if it was true that 'the charge of attempting to murder Constable Fitzgerald was an untruthful one it was perfectly idle to say that this would justify the prisoner in subsequently killing Constable Lonigan because he was engaged in the duty of searching for the Kelly gang'.

Bindon spoke for a considerable time, pointing out (as has already been stated) to the jury, in the common fashion of the day, that his client's mouth was sealed — 'but if he could be sworn then he would give a totally different version of the transaction' (The *Argus,* 30 October 1880). The only important evidence was that of Constable McIntyre. They should remember, Bindon urged, that McIntyre was not to be regarded as a witness worthy of entire credit; he must have been anything but cool at the time. He could not remember, as he now purported to remember, in such fine detail and with such consecutive precision the sudden events of that day in 1878. He left them with the remark that he trusted if they had 'the smallest doubt . . . the jury would give a verdict in the case different from that which the Crown expected' (The *Argus,* 30 October 1880).

In Sir Redmond Barry's charge to the jury there is a significant omission. He told them, and it was undoubtedly in his own discretion, that he would *not* go through the evidence because it was so fresh in the jury's mind. The judge confined himself to defining for them the felony of murder. '. . . The counsel for the defence had also told the jury to receive the evidence of McIntyre with very great caution, but he would go further, and hope that the jury would receive and weigh all evidence with caution. It was not necessary to have McIntyre's evidence corroborated, and he asked the jury to note the behaviour of McIntyre in the witness-box, and say whether his conduct was that of a man who wanted to deceive. . . . Counsel for the defence said that the prisoner's mouth was closed, and that if it was not closed he could tell a different story to the one told by McIntyre. But the fact was that the prisoner's mouth was not closed. That he could not give sworn testimony was true, but he could have made a statement which, if consistent with his conduct for the last eighteen months, would have been entitled to every consideration; but the prisoner had not done so. . . . The jury would, however, have to regard the evidence as a whole, and accordingly say whether the murder had been committed. It could not be manslaughter. The verdict of the jury must either be guilty of murder or an acquittal' (The *Argus,* 30 October 1880).

At 5.10 p.m., Sir Redmond Barry finished his charge and the jury left the Court. They returned half an hour later and delivered their unanimous verdict: that Edward Kelly was guilty of the wilful murder of Thomas Lonigan.

It was and is still the practice that when a man has been convicted of a felony he is addressed by the Judge's Associate and asked:

What have you to say, why the Court should not pass sentence [*if capital, add* of death] upon you.[14]

This question, called the *allocutus,* is usually answered today, if answered at all, by some assertion of innocence or some statement in mitigation. In former times it was the occasion for clerics, convicted of serious crimes, to plead benefit of clergy. When benefit of clergy became generally available to all who were literate, and then to any one who could recite the first verse of Psalm 51 *'Miserere mei, deus',*

---

[14] See Gurner, *op. cit.,* p. 58.

the *allocutus* was the opportunity for this demonstration.[15] Benefit of clergy is gone but the *allocutus* remains.[16] Kelly made extraordinary use of his opportunity (The *Argus,* 30 October 1880):

> Well, it is rather late for me to speak now. I tried to do so this morning, but I thought afterwards that I had better not. No one understands my case as I do, and I almost wish now that I had spoken; not that I fear death. On the evidence that has been given, no doubt, the jury or any other jury could not give any other verdict. But it is on account of the witnesses, and with their evidence, no different verdict could be given. No one knows anything about my case but myself. Mr Bindon knows nothing about it at all, and Mr Gaunson knows nothing, though they have tried to do their best for me. I'm sorry I did not ask my counsel to sit down, and examine the witnesses myself. I could have made things look different, I'm sure. No one understands my case.

When he had finished the Crier made his dread proclamation:

> Oyez, oyez, oyez. All manner of persons are commanded to keep silence whilst sentence of death is passed upon the prisoner at the bar, upon pain of imprisonment.[17]

And then there occurred one of the most extraordinary episodes in the history of the administration of the criminal law in Victoria. Barry J. addressed the now convicted murderer, but what was intended as a homily became a colloquy, so unexpected that it was taken down in direct

---

[15] Benefit of clergy was wholly abolished in England by section 6 of the *Criminal Law Act, 1827.* Its abolition in the colony of New South Wales was effected in 1828 by the Act 9 Geo. IV, No. 1.

[16] Its omission does not impugn the validity of a conviction; see *R* v. *Gombos* [1965] 1 W.L.R. 575.

[17] See Gurner, *op. cit.,* p. 58.

speech by the reporters present and reproduced entirely (The *Argus*, 30 October 1880).

*His Honour:* Edward Kelly, the verdict is one which you must have fully expected.

*Prisoner:* Under the circumstances, I did expect this verdict.

*His Honour:* No circumstances that I can conceive could here control the verdict.

*Prisoner:* Perhaps if you had heard me examine the witness, you might understand. I could do it.

*His Honour:* I will even give you credit for the skill which you desire to show you possess.

*Prisoner:* I don't say this out of flashness. I do not recognize myself as a great man; but it is quite possible for me to clear myself of this charge if I liked to do so. If I desired to do it, I could have done so in spite of anything attempted against me.

*His Honour:* The facts against you are so numerous and so conclusive, not only as regards the offence which you are now charged with, but also for the long series of criminal acts which you have committed during the last eighteen months, that I do not think any rational person could have arrived at any other conclusion. The verdict of the jury was irresistible, and there could not be any doubt about its being a right verdict. I have no right or wish to inflict upon you any personal remarks. It is painful in the extreme to perform the duty which I have now to discharge, and I will confine myself strictly to do it. I do not think that anything I could say would aggravate the pain you must now be suffering.

*Prisoner:* No; I declare before you and my God that my mind is as easy and clear as it possibly can be. (Sensation.)

*His Honour:* It is blasphemous of you to say so.

*Prisoner:* I do not fear death, and I am the last man in the world to take a man's life away. I believe that two years ago, before this thing happened, if a man pointed a gun at me to shoot me, I should not have stopped him, so careful was

121

I of taking life. I am not a murderer, but if there is innocent life at stake, then I say I must take some action. If I
see innocent life taken, I should certainly shoot if I was
forced to do so, but I should first want to know whether
this could not be prevented, but I should have to do it if it
could not be stopped in any other way.

*His Honour:* Your statement involves wicked and criminal
reflection of untruth upon the witnesses who have given
evidence.

*Prisoner:* I dare say the day will come when we shall all
have to go to a bigger court than this. Then we will see
who is right and who is wrong. As regards anything about
myself, all I care for is that my mother, who is now in
prison, shall not have it to say that she reared a son who
could not have altered this charge if he had liked to do so.

*His Honour:* An offence of the kind which you stand
accused of is not of an ordinary character. There are many
murders which have been discovered and committed in
this colony under different circumstances, but none show
greater atrocity than those you committed. These crimes
proceed from different motives. Some arise from a sordid
desire to take from others the property which they acquired
or inherited, some from jealousy, some from a bare desire
to thieve, but this crime was an enormity out of all proportion. A party of men took up arms against society, organized
as it was for mutual protection and regard for the law.

*Prisoner:* Yes, that is the way the evidence brought it out.

*His Honour:* Unfortunately, in a new community, where
society was not bound together so closely as it should be,
there was a class which looked upon the perpetrators of
these crimes as heroes. But these unfortunate, ill-educated,
ill-prompted youths must be taught to consider the value
of human life. It could hardly be believed that a man would
sacrifice the life of his fellow-creatures in this wild manner.
The idea was enough to make one shudder in thinking of
it. The end of your companions was comparatively a better
termination than the miserable death which awaits you. It
is remarkable that although New South Wales had joined

Victoria in offering a large reward for the detection of the gang, no person was found to discover it. There seemed to be a spell cast over the people of this particular district, which I can only attribute either to sympathy with crime or dread of the consequences of doing their duty. For months the country has been disturbed by you and your associates, and you have actually had the hardihood to confess to having stolen two hundred horses.

*Prisoner:* Who proves this?

*His Honour:* That is your own statement.

*Prisoner:* You have not heard me; if I had examined the witnesses, I could have brought it out differently.

*His Honour:* I am not accusing you. This statement has been made several times by the witnesses. You confessed it to them and you stand self-accused. It is also proved that you committed several attacks upon the banks, and you seem to have appropriated large sums of money — several thousands of pounds. It has also come within my knowledge that the country has expended about £50,000 in consequence of the acts of which you and your party have been guilty. Although we have had such examples as Clarke, Gardiner, Melville, Morgan and Scott, who have all met ignominious deaths, still the effect has, apparently, not been to hinder others from following in their footsteps. I think that this is much to be deplored, and some steps must be taken to have society protected. Your unfortunate and miserable associates have met with deaths which you might envy. I will forward to the Executive the notes of the evidence which I have taken and all circumstances connected with your case, but I cannot hold out any hope to you that the sentence which I am now about to pass will be remitted. I desire not to give you any further pain or to aggravate the distressing feelings which you must be enduring.

His Honour then passed sentence of death, and concluded with the usual formula: 'May the Lord have mercy on your soul.'

*Prisoner:* Yes, I will meet you there.

And with what was to prove a prophetic utterance, the trial of Kelly ended.

Efforts were made by David Gaunson, Kelly's attorney, his brother William, and Hamilton, Chairman of the Society for the Abolition of Capital Punishment, and members of Kelly's family, to procure a commutation of the sentence of death. The Gaunsons and Hamilton formed what the *Argus* referred to as the Reprieve Committee and their efforts were reported in detail in the papers. There were public meetings and a petition seeking mercy, signed by many thousands, was presented to the Governor of Victoria. But all these efforts failed. Kelly was hanged on 11 November 1880, in the Melbourne Jail, Russell Street.

## KELLY'S DEFENCE

As I have said already, Kelly's defence rested on Bindon's cross-examination of the Crown witnesses and on his final address to the jury. In another very real sense it also rested on Sir Redmond Barry's charge to the jury. It is always the trial judge's duty to put the whole defence of an accused person to the jury as completely and fairly as possible. Indeed, there are a number of cases in which appellate tribunals have quashed convictions because a particular defence which was open to an accused person on the facts adduced in evidence has not been put to the jury, even though that defence was not adopted or pressed by the accused himself during the trial.

The Crown's case was summed up by Smyth when he said:

It [Kelly's motive for killing Lonigan] was one of the malignant hatred of the police because the person had been leading a wild, lawless life and was at war with society. He had proved abundantly, by the witnesses produced for the Crown, who were practically not cross-examined, that the murder of Lonigan was committed in cold blood. (The *Age,* 30 October 1880.)

Smyth it was who first referred to Kelly's line of defence, prefacing his statement with the contemptuous aside 'so far as he could gather anything from the cross-examination. . . .' He mentioned the Fitzpatrick case, the treatment of Kelly's family as a result, what he said was referred to as a justification for revenge on the police, and the point that because Kennedy and his men did not surrender the gang was justified in what was called 'defending themselves. Would the jury allow this state of affairs to exist? Such a thing was not to be tolerated and he had almost to apologise to the jury for discussing the matter.' (The *Age,* 30 October 1880.)

This is one of a number of statements which appear in the reports in the newspapers which show that though in form Kelly was being tried only for the murder of Constable Lonigan, in fact the whole episode in the Wombat Ranges, comprehending the killings of Constable Scanlon and Sergeant Kennedy as well, was considered as if there was one all-embracing indictment against Kelly. Despite his expressed scorn for its merit, Smyth was concerned that Kelly's defence might affect the jury and somehow erode the Crown's towering indictment.

Even admitting the prisoner's defence, that the charge of attempting to murder Constable Fitzpatrick was an untruthful one, it was perfectly idle to say that this would justify the prisoner in killing Constable Lonigan because he was engaged upon the duty of searching for the Kelly gang. (The *Age,* 30 October 1880.)

His concern was, of course, groundless.

Something has already been said about Bindon's final address to the jury, and of his attack in it upon McIntyre's recollection of events then two years old, and his hint at the possibility of bias feeding memory. In it he repeated his complaints about the introduction of evidence concerning events after the death of Lonigan and reminded the jury of Kelly's incompetence as a witness. He never put clearly or coherently that defence which had seemed apparent to the Crown Prosecutor. There are a few sentences scattered through the report published in The *Age* which refer to it.

> . . . [H]e would point out that the police had appeared on the scene, not in uniform, but in plain clothes, and armed to the teeth. . . . Because the Kellys were found in the bush, it did not follow that they were secreting themselves; on the contrary they were following their ordinary occupation in this part of the country when they fell in with this armed party of men. The Kellys did not know who these people were, and it was a most dangerous doctrine to raise on the evidence of one man more especially when the charge was that one man shot another deliberately and in cold blood. (The *Age*, 30 October 1880.)

Bindon suggested that the *identity* of Lonigan's killer was uncertain. This was presumably a thinly veiled invitation to the jury to find that Lonigan had been killed by one of Kelly's companions and a further suggestion that in those circumstances Kelly was entitled to be acquitted.

Sir Redmond Barry's summing up was, by today's standards, brief, and would be considered unsatisfactory. As has been said, he did not review the evidence but concerned himself with describing parts of that legal framework within which the search for the truth was to be undertaken by the jury.

Firstly he stated the established rule that if several men planned to murder another, then not only the actual killer but also his confederates, who were there ready to assist, were equally guilty of murder.[18] He reminded the jury that Kelly could have made an unsworn statement. Then he pointed out to them how important was McIntyre's statement, and that they might accept it though it was uncorroborated.

Insofar as the judge put what Smyth had referred to as Kelly's defence to the jury, he spoke of it thus:

. . . [If] four men went out armed intending to resist those in lawful pursuit of an object, and one of these four men interfered with those in their lawful business, and killed them, the four would be equally guilty of murder, and might be executed. Here four constables went out to perform a duty. It was said they were in plain clothes. But with that they had nothing to do. Regard them as civilians — he used the word because it had been made use of in the course of the trial, although he thought it inappropriate — what right had four other men armed to stop them? . . . [W]hat right had the prisoner and three other men to desire them to hold up their hands and surrender? But there was another state of things which was not to be disregarded. These men were persons charged with a responsible, and, as it turned out, a dangerous duty and they were aware of that before they started. They went in pursuit of two persons [Ned and Dan Kelly] who had been gazetted as persons against whom warrants were issued [see the reference to the evidence of Detective Ward p. 115], and they were in lawful discharge of their duty when in pursuit of these two persons; therefore they had a double protection — that of the ordinary citizen, and of being ministers of the law, executive officers of the administra-

[18] Not as 'principals in the first degree', as the report in the *Age*, 30 October 1880 reads, but as principals in the second degree. Sir Redmond Barry did not instruct the jury that it must first be sure that such a plan was made between the four members of the Kelly gang before applying these rules in these circumstances. But see *Mohan* v. *R.* [1967] 2 W.L.R. 676.

tion of the peace of the country. Whether they were in uniform or not there was no privilege on the part of any person to molest them, and still less was there power or authority to molest them as constables. [The *Argus,* 30 October 1880.]

There was but one other statement concerning the defence made by Barry. The evidence of what had occurred after the death of Lonigan was admitted by him because the jury might infer from it what was the motive for shooting Lonigan, or whether the shooting was accidental or in self-defence.

It is clear that Sir Redmond Barry considered that there was no real merit in a plea of self-defence put forward on Kelly's behalf. The whole tenor of his statements to the jury set out above reveals his undoubtedly clear view that the Crown's evidence established what it asserted; a cold-blooded killing by one of a group of four men who had agreed together to fall upon the police party with lethal violence. It is my purpose to consider whether there was any more substance to Kelly's defence than was allowed by the trial judge.

By 1880 it was very clearly established that if a man killed another who had made or threatened to make a violent attack upon him then the killing might not be murder. The killing could be justified or excused in those circumstances, even if it was intentional. It was necessary to establish, of course, that the killing was in good faith for the purposes of self-defence and not 'malice coloured under pretence of necessity'.[19] Furthermore the intentional killing was only excused if it was *necessary* in the circumstances for the killer to use deadly violence to protect himself. Sir James Stephen, a judge of the High Court of Justice and the most famous writer on criminal law in nineteenth-century England, stated part of this doctrine as

---

[19] Hawkins, *Pleas of the Crown* (8th ed., 1824), p. 79. The expression is repeated by Lowe, J., in the modern Victorian case of *R.* v. *McKay* [1957] V.R. 560, 562.

follows: 'If a person is assaulted in such a manner as to put him in immediate and obvious danger of instant death or grievous bodily harm, he may defend himself on the spot and may kill or wound the person by whom he was assaulted.'[20]

In his statement of this justification or excuse for intentional killing, Stephen maintained, on the authority of the famous institutional writers of the seventeenth and eighteenth centuries, that the killer would be exculpated where he inflicted 'no greater injury in any case than he in good faith and on reasonable grounds believes to be necessary'. The law in the Australian colonies was the same as that which had been expounded by Stephen as the law of England.

But in 1870, the Supreme Court of New South Wales decided the case of *The Queen* v. *Griffin*.[21] The presiding judge was another Stephen, Sir Alfred of that name, Chief Justice of the Supreme Court of New South Wales.

It was clear in that case that Griffin had fatally shot his neighbour Londergan. Both were farmers and there had been a series of quarrels between them about real or supposed trespasses. The dead man had shot a pig belonging to Griffin who had then shot one of his neighbour's. When Londergan heard of this he became very angry and ran towards Griffin's house. Griffin, who had a gun in his hand, called him to stop, and he did; minutes later Griffin fired and killed Londergan. There was evidence that Londergan was a man of many 'violent tempers and habits', while Griffin was 'ordinarily a quiet and inoffensive person'. Griffin was convicted of murder and the trial judge, Hargrave J., reserved a special case for the consideration of the Full Court. The Full Court decided that Griffin's conviction must be quashed, Hargrave J. dissenting.

[20] *A Digest of the Criminal Law* (6th ed., 1904), p. 159.
[21] 10 S.C.R. (N.S.W.) 91. This case heralded the now clearly established modern doctrine, particularly the doctrine of excessive self-defence. See *R.* v. *Howe* (1958) 100 C.L.R. 448; *R.* v. *Tikos* (No. 1 and No. 2), [1963] V.R. 285, 306.

In his judgement, Stephen C.J. said:

> It was contended, therefore, that under the circum-
> stances, the prisoner reasonably believed, and at all events
> *really did believe*[22] that the deceased was about to inflict
> serious bodily injury on him, and that he could not
> otherwise protect himself from the meditated violence.
> Now the law clearly is, that if there was in fact such a
> design manifested, on the part of the deceased — an
> intention then and there to commit the act of violence
> suspected, or said to have been, by either wounding or
> inflicting other grievous bodily harm on the prisoner —
> or even, as I apprehend, *if there was at the moment
> reasonable ground for believing that such a design exis-
> ted*[23]— the prisoner was entitled immediately to take
> effectual measures for his protection; and, being in his
> own house, was not bound to retreat in order to avoid
> the danger. The person so believing could not indeed
> justify the taking of life, or using a deadly weapon in a
> manner likely to take life, unless he could not otherwise
> prevent the apprehended injury — or, at least, unless
> there was reasonable ground for believing that there
> were no other means, and he did in truth act on that
> belief. I do not say, that in each case alike the homicide
> (supposing death to ensue) would be justifiable. *In one
> of the cases put, the act of killing might be manslaughter.*
> But in none of them would it be murder.[24]

The emphasized expressions are particularly important
in two respects. The first two clearly reveal that it is the
accused's behaviour which is in question, not the innocence
or otherwise of his victim. If he believes that he is being
approached or threatened, then he may not be a murderer;
the rider of reasonableness means that his belief must be
one which other men in his circumstances might entertain.
The last expression is taken today to refer to the situation
where the accused's response is excessive, where he goes

[22], [23] and [24] Author's italics.

too far in resisting the real or supposed attack. His guilt is mitigated because of his own appreciation, distorted though it is in the eyes of later investigators of the situation.[25]

This is a very different expression of the law from that found in the charge of Sir Redmond Barry. It is particularly significant to contrast the last part of Stephen C.J.'s statement of the law with Barry's unequivocal assertion to the jury that they could not find Kelly guilty of manslaughter, that it was murder or nothing. Stephen C.J. is credited today with applying what we now refer to as the rule of qualified self-defence to a charge of murder. Today the doctrine has been very clearly enunciated by the High Court of Australia in *R. v. Howe*[26] where the Court said, approving the statement made by Lowe J. in *R. v. McKay* a year earlier[27], that: 'If the occasion warrants action in self-defence . . . but the person taking action acts beyond the necessity of the occasion and kills the offender, the crime is manslaughter — not murder.'

But of course, it may be said that the obvious difference between *R. v. Griffin* and *R. v. Kelly* lies in the character of the victim. Griffin deals with self-defence between man and man; what relevance has it to the case of man and policeman acting in the course of duty? So, before turning to look at some aspects of the evidence to see whether it could be inferred that Kelly really had an apprehension of imminent danger to himself, something must be said about the position of the police, to which Sir Redmond Barry referred at some length in this charge.

By 1880 the law extended a particular protection to its officers and to those engaged in its enforcement. It continues so to do. The protection is two-fold. One part is oblique; any person who unintentionally kills an officer of the law while resisting or escaping a lawful arrest is

---

[25] See P. Brett and P. L. Waller, *Cases and Materials in Criminal Law* (2nd ed., 1965), pp. 201-25, esp. 205-9, where the judgment of Dixon, C.J. in *Howe's Case* is set out. See C. Howard, *Australian Criminal Law* (1965), p. 80, n. 42.

[26] (1958) 100 C.L.R. 448.

[27] [1957] V.R. 560.

NED KELLY: MAN AND MYTH

guilty of murder.[28] This kind of murder is called construc-
tive, in that it is not necessary for the prosecution to prove
malice aforethought in the sense of an intention to kill or
an intention to cause grievous bodily harm, denominated
'express malice'. The other part is direct. Stephen put it
thus:

> The intentional infliction of death or bodily harm is not
> a crime when it is done . . . by a constable, or other
> officer of justice, in order to execute the warrant of arrest
> for treason or felony; which cannot otherwise be execu-
> ted, although the person named in the warrant offers no
> violence to any person; provided . . . that the object for
> which death or harm is inflicted cannot be otherwise
> accomplished.[29]

This protection is only afforded where the arrest is lawful.
It is clear that the primary object of officers of the law is
arrest. It is only if the *arrest* cannot be otherwise effected
that death or bodily harm may be inflicted. In the usual
case, such behaviour will only be lawful if the police efforts
at arrest are met with violent resistance, despite Stephen's
statement to the contrary. There are a number of nineteenth-century cases in which killers of police constables
were acquitted, or only convicted of manslaughter when
tried for murder, because the police were proceeding on
illegal warrants, or because for some other reason, the arrest
was regarded as illegal. In one, for example, a parish constable attempted an arrest in a strange parish where he had
no jurisdiction.[30] This rule affords no protection to police
who used an opportunity offered by the issue of a warrant
of arrest to hunt down and kill the person named in that
warrant. That would be a clear instance of what Hawkins
described, in the context of self-defence, as 'malice coloured
under pretence of necessity'.

[28] See, e.g., *R.* v. *Ryan & Walker* [1966] V.R. 533, esp. at 564.
[29] *A Digest of the Criminal Law* (6th ed., 1904), p. 158-9.
[30] See, e.g., *R.* v. *Phelps* (1841) C. & M. 180 and *R.* v. *Dadson* (1850)
2 Den. 35.

The modern case of *Trobridge* v. *Hardy*[31] decided by the High Court in 1955, underscores this notion that the police are only protected when they are acting with an honest intention of enforcing, vindicating or giving effect to the law. The circumstances in this case are entirely different from Kelly's. But in it Fullagar and Kitto J. both denied that a Western Australian police constable could avail himself of the protection of a specific statutory provision. That provision was cast in very wide terms, but the judges held that it only afforded protection from civil suit if the constable had done what he did to the plaintiff to 'vindicate and give effect to the law', and not 'wantonly and in abuse of his authority'. In the judgements there are references to and considerations of a number of English cases of a like kind wherein the same approach is manifested. In one such case, Scrutton L.J. stated that the officer is not acting in pursuance of a statute or carrying into effect a statute, whatever he may acually do, if what he has done is not 'done in intended execution of a statute but only in pretended execution thereof.'[32] And lest it be still thought that the citizen may never lawfully defend himself against the police, a case decided by the English Divisional Court only a few months ago points out very strongly that this is not so. In *Kenlin* v. *Gardiner*[33] the Divisional Court decided that self-defence was available as an answer to a charge of assaulting the police, *as in the case of any other assault,* if it was shown that a prior assault by the police (the occasion for the self-defence) was not itself justified by considerations of law-enforcement.

It is against this background, briefly sketched, that Kelly's defence may be viewed. It is not possible to relate in detail all the evidence referring to Kelly's beliefs which was adduced in the trial, but some of it will be set out, together with supporting statements in the documents

---

[31] (1955) 94 C.L.R. 147.
[32] *G. Scammell and Nephew Ltd.* v. *Hurley* [1929] 1 K.B. 419, 427.
[33] [1967] 2 W.L.R. 129.

referred to as the Cameron Letter and the Jerilderie Letter, which are attributed to Kelly.[34]

Here is the picture in outline. Kelly believed that Constable Fitzpatrick had sworn a false information about the events at Greta, and as a result that he was quite falsely accused of a capital felony, wounding Fitzpatrick with intent to murder him.[35] Furthermore he believed that the police who came to execute the warrant of arrest, issued as a result of Fitzpatrick's information, came not to apprehend him but to shoot him dead on sight. He thought that he was to be hunted down, not arrested and brought to trial. Kelly's beliefs in this regard appear as part of his admissions which were related by several of the witnesses at the trial.

They are most clearly set out in the two documents which have just been referred to which were not admitted in evidence, though the Jerilderie Letter was tendered at the close of Living's testimony.[36] It is clear that the exculpatory parts of these admissions were properly moved in evidence, despite their 'self-serving' character. The jury was entitled to treat them as evidence of the truth of the statements there made. A great nineteenth-century judge said: '. . . if the prosecution makes the prisoner's declaration evidence, it then becomes evidence for the prisoner as well as against him.'[37]

---

[34] I have used the text of the Cameron letter set out in *Ned Kelly, Being His Own Story of His Life and Crimes,* Introduction by Clive Turnbull (Melbourne, 1942).
Turnbull wrote: 'The letter now published was written at the time of the Euroa robbery and addressed to Mr Donald Cameron M.L.A. Posted at Glenrowan on December 14, 1878, the letter was delivered at Parliament House, Melbourne and handed over to the Government.'
The Jerilderie Letter is published as an appendix to Max Brown, *Australian Son. The Story of Ned Kelly* (1948), pp. 272-83.

[35] Wounding with intent to murder remained a capital felony in Victoria until 1949.

[36] See, *Argus,* 30 October 1880: 'Prisoner gave me [Living] a statement. He afterwᵃᵈⁱs handed it to the police. . . . Statement was tendered in evidᵉⁿce but was not received.'

[37] *Per* Parke b. in *R.* v. *Higgins* (1829) 3 C. & P. 603, 604.

A few extracts will serve to reveal these beliefs. In McIntyre's evidence, he stated that after Lonigan was killed, Kelly called him over.

> We had some conversation, in which the prisoner expressed a belief that the police had come out to shoot him. . . . He said, 'What gun is this? Is it a breach loader?' I said, 'Yes, it is.' He said, 'That looks very like as if you came out to shoot me.' I said, 'You can't blame the men, they have got their duty to do, and they must come out as they are ordered.' He said, 'They are not ordered to go about the country shooting people.' He then said, 'What became of the Sydney man?' — he referred to a man who murdered Sergeant Wallins [*sic*] in New South Wales. I said, 'He was shot by the police.' He said, 'If the police shot him they shot the wrong man. I suppose if you could you would shoot me some day, but before you do I shall make some of you suffer for it. That fellow Fitzpatrick is the cause of all this.' (The *Argus*, 29 October 1880.)

In cross-examination, Gloster, the draper, stated: 'Prisoner said he was 200 miles away at the time of the alleged shooting at Greta . . .' (The *Argus*, 29 October 1880.)

A similar statement was repeated by Constable Richards in his evidence in chief (The *Argus*, 30 October 1880.) Similar statements are made in the Cameron and Jerilderie Letters, in both of which the writer states that Dan Kelly distracted Fitzpatrick by saying, 'Ned is coming now,' and then took him in a wrestling hold and threw him out of the door. In the Jerilderie Letter Kelly expresses his fears thus:

> . . . So I came back to Victoria, knew I would get no justice if I gave myself up . . . Heard about the police used to be blowing off that they would not ask me to stand, they would shoot me first then cry surrender. . . . Superintendent Smith used to say to my sisters see all the men I have out today I will have as many more out

135

tomorrow and we will blow him into pieces as small as
paper that is in our guns . . .[38]

It may be argued, therefore, that the jury could have found
that Kelly had a real belief, and one which might be
characterized (in the language of Stephen C.J.'s judgement
in *R. v. Griffin*) as held on reasonable grounds, that he was
going to be the victim of an unlawful and violent attack,
not the subject of a lawful arrest. It is in this kind of setting
that the actual shooting of Lonigan should be examined,
and the stories of the two men who lived to tell of it considered.

In his evidence McIntyre stated:

Lonigan alone was armed, and he only had a revolver in
his belt. He and Lonigan were not shot at from ambush;
voices called out, 'Bail up; hold up your hands'. Lonigan
was in my rear and to my left. Saw the prisoner move his
rifle, bringing it in a line with Lonigan, and fire (The
*Argus*, 29 October 1880.)

Kelly maintained always that he shot at Lonigan because
Lonigan made for cover behind a log and tried to draw his
revolver. George Stephens, in his evidence, repeated what
Kelly told him at Faithfull's Creek Station near Euroa.

Prisoner said: We were behind a log. I told Dan to cover
Lonigan and I would cover McIntyre. I then called on
them to throw up their hands and McIntyre immediately
did so. Lonigan made for the log, and tried to draw the
revolver as he went along. He laid down behind the log,
and rested his revolver on the top of the log and covered
Dan. I then took my rifle off McIntyre and fired at
Lonigan, grazing his temple. Lonigan then disappeared
below the log, but gradually rose again, and as he did so
I fired again and shot him through the head. (The
*Argus*, 29 October 1880.)

[38] Brown, *op. cit.*, pp. 277-8.

In the Cameron letter Kelly gave his version at greater length:

> ... [O]n the 26th October I came on the tracks of Police horses, between Table Top and the Bogs, I crossed there and went to Emu Swamp and returning home came on more police tracks making for our camp. I told my mates and me and my brother went out next morning and found police camped at the Shingle Hut with long fire arms and we came to the conclusion our doom was sealed unless we could take their fire-arms, as we had nothing but a gun and a rifle if they came on us at our work or camp. We had no chance only to die like dogs as we thought the country was woven with police and we might have a chance of fighting them if we had fire-arms, as it generally takes 40 to 1. We approached the Spring as close as we could get to the camp, the intervening space being clear. We saw two men at the log, they got up and one took a double barrel fowling piece and one drove the horses down and hobbled them, against the tent and we thought there was more men in the tent, those being on sentry. We could have shot those two men, without speaking, but not wishing to take life we waited. McIntyre laid the gun against the stump and Lonigan sat on the log. I advanced, my brother Dan keeping McIntyre covered. I called on them to throw up their hands McIntyre obeyed and never attempted to reach for his gun or revolver. Lonigan ran to a battery of logs and put his head up to take aim at me, when I shot him, or he would have shot me, as I knew well.

McIntyre's sworn testimony at the trial of Lonigan's behaviour might have been sharply contradicted by Bindon. He could have put to him the statements he made almost immediately after his successful escape to Mansfield. His statements are preserved in the State Archives. In the statement he made to Sub-Inspector Pewtress he said:

Suddenly and without us being aware of their approach four men with rifles presented at us called us to 'bail up hold up your hands.' I being disarmed at the time did so, Constable Lonigan made a motion towards his rifle which he was carrying.[39]

When he came to make his statement at the magisterial inquiry, held at Mansfield before Alexander Pilcher J.P., on 29 October 1878, McIntyre said Constable Lonigan endeavoured to get behind a tree three or four yards off. Before he could do so he was shot.[39a]

In his various statements while he was an outlaw running from the police, Kelly seems always to have adhered to the story that Lonigan ran towards a battery of logs, dropped behind them, and was lifting his head to take aim with his revolver when he was shot. This was a very different narration of the events than was provided at the trial by McIntyre, and it might have been one which the jury, properly charged about self-defence, would have found acceptable. It would have been for them to decide, in those circumstances, whether Kelly's act in shooting at Lonigan then was really necessary in order to preserve his own life, it being remembered that Kelly believed that these were not policemen out to make a lawful arrest but men intent on shooting him down. The jury might have shared the view that David Gaunson, his attorney, expressed at the clemency meeting which was held at the Hippodrome: 'Kelly was not morally guilty of murder as he was under a belief that the police went out to shoot him instead of arresting him when the murder(s) of Lonigan . . . took place.' (The *Age*, 6 November 1880.)

These views have been expressed only in respect of the killing of Lonigan, the man with whose murder Kelly was charged and in respect of whose murder he was convicted. It would be impossible to make out a similar argument in respect of Sergeant Kennedy, if one believes the admissions

[39] By 'rifle' McIntyre must have meant 'revolver'.
[39a] See p. 142, *post*.

Gloster swore Kelly made. 'I did not wish to leave him to be torn up by wild beasts while dying. I thought it more humane to shoot him.'[40]

What Kelly regarded as his humane intentions, in those circumstances, would constitute no defence at all to a charge of wilful and deliberate murder. But he was not tried in respect of that killing, possibly because McIntyre had galloped off on Sergeant Kennedy's horse before Kennedy was killed. He could not give that eye- and ear-witness testimony which he was able to give for the Crown in respect of the killing of Lonigan.

It cannot be stated with dogmatic certainty that, had the defence which has been outlined above been fairly put to the jury, and those facts which appear in the evidence related to it (and, perhaps, McIntyre's evidence shaken by revealing his prior inconsistent statements of October 1878), that Kelly would have been acquitted altogether or only convicted of manslaughter. It would have been the jury's task to decide a number of difficult questions going to Kelly's beliefs about what the police planned to do, about the necessity of protecting himself by holding up the police and ordering them to surrender, and then about the necessity of shooting at a resisting Lonigan — if they found he had been about to fire his revolver.

There were some contradictory admissions made by Kelly which were proved by McIntyre, Senior Constable Kelly and Sergeant Steele. McIntyre testified that, after the Glenrowan fight, he had seen the wounded Kelly and said:

> Why did you come near us at all. You knew who we were and could have easily kept out of the way? *Prisoner:* You'd soon have found us out and if we didn't shoot you, you'd have shot us. Besides we had bad horses they were poor, and had firearms, we wanted to make a rise.[41]

Senior Constable Kelly also spoke about a conversation

[40] *Notes of Evidence*, p. 65.
[41] *Notes of Evidence*, p. 38.

with Kelly after Glenrowan. 'He asked for a drink. I gave him some milk and water. I said, 'Ned, it's all up now. What about Fitzpatrick's statement?' Prisoner said, 'His statement is correct, I shot him.'[42] Sergeant Steele corroborated this last admission. If these admissions are accepted as true they cut the ground away in large measure from beneath the structure which has been erected.

It is difficult to assert with confidence, on the basis of staccato Notes of Evidence and reports in newspapers which did not purport to produce a complete transcript of the trial, that a particular state of facts has been established or that a particular hypothesis has been shown to be completely unfounded. A gap of eighty-seven years is no narrow chasm to cross. Last year an English judge, conducting an inquiry into a case which had been tried in 1950, said:

> Stale evidence is often bad evidence. Experience shows that it does not take long for human recollections to fail. When this happens it means that valuable evidence is either partly or wholly lost. When recollection begins to fail imagination often takes its place. . . . It can happen that what is spoken about as relevant is in the main but make-believe. It sometimes happens that contemporaneous documents act as a reliable check against human recollections and they will often be more trustworthy than the memory of a witness. They serve as a record of events, but with the passage of time, it may not be possible to detect mistakes in written documents, so that one that was apparently accurate becomes the more misleading.[43]

The point of these remarks is obvious. So, perhaps, the last word must be Kelly's:

[42] Notes of Evidence, p. 88.
[43] The Case of Timothy John Evans. Report of an Inquiry by the Hon Mr Justice Brabin. Cmnd. 3101, 1966, pp. 5-6.

*His Honour:* Your statement involves a cruelly wicked charge of perjury against a phalanx of witnesses.

*The Prisoner:* I dare say, that a day will come, at a bigger Court than this, when we shall see which is right and which is wrong. (The *Argus*, 30 October 1880.)

## SOURCES AND ACKNOWLEDGEMENTS

The three Melbourne daily newspapers of the time, the *Age,* the *Argus* and the *Herald,* each published lengthy accounts of Kelly's trial. I have used the accounts which appeared in the *Age* and the *Argus.*

Longhand 'Notes of Evidence' were taken at the trial. These Notes were sent to the Governor of Victoria, for consideration by the Executive Council, after Kelly was convicted and sentenced to death. I am grateful to the Crown Law Department for providing me with a photostat copy of this material, which I have used extensively in conjunction with the newspaper reports.

The Crown Law Department's files on the Kelly affair are now lodged in the State Archives of Victoria. The brief prepared for the Crown Prosecutor, containing the depositions taken before the Magistrate at Beechworth, form part of these files. Among them are also original and copy warrants, reports, affidavits and notes relating to the whole period of the Kelly outbreak. I am grateful to the State Archivist, and to members of his staff, for their help in making this material available.

My exposition of the criminal process in Victoria in 1880 has been based in part on Henry F. Gurner's *Principles of the Criminal Law of the Colony of Victoria* (1871). Gurner was Crown Solicitor of Victoria when he wrote this book and when Kelly was tried; his name appears on the Crown Prosecutor's brief.

There is some valuable material in the 'Reports of the Royal Commission into the Kelly Outbreak'. The Commission delivered five reports between its appointment in 1881 and 1883; the First Progress Report, the Second Report, the Ad Interim Report, the Special (Detective) Report, and the Final Report. These are all to be found in the Parliamentary Papers of the Legislative Assembly of Victoria published between 1881-4.

*Ian Jones:* In preparing the account of the death of Lonigan given by Kelly and Constable McIntyre, you are possibly not aware of an account given by McIntyre to Superintendent Sadleir two days after Glenrowan and quoted verbatim by Sadleir in his *Recollections of a Victorian Police Officer*.

In this, McIntyre's account of the shooting of Lonigan tallies exactly with that given by Ned Kelly. He claims that Lonigan drew his revolver, ran to a log, got behind the log and was coming up to fire when he was shot by Ned Kelly. This of course, clashes with every other account given by McIntyre. At the trial, during the examination of Snr. Const. Kelly, Kelly describes the incident between himself, McIntyre, and Ned Kelly. He said McIntyre said, 'You had my chest covered with a rifle, and then you turned around and shot Lonigan'.

The prisoner said, 'No, Lonigan was behind a log with his revolver pointed at me and I shot him.' Sadleir suggests that McIntyre committed perjury at Kelly's trial and in all sworn statements in connection with the murder of Lonigan subsequent to the account he gave to Sadleir.

*Professor Waller:* I am not going to commit myself on whether or not he committed perjury. But what could have been done at Kelly's trial (and what so often is done), is to put to a vital witness what are called his previous inconsistent statements. Now there are other explanations beside the dreadful explanation of perjury. His mind may have become clearer. He may have forgotten, though that is very unlikely. But, as far as the accused is concerned, he is entitled to have the jury know that a witness has not always told the same story. That is why counsel is so anxious to find discrepancies between what is recorded in the depositions taken at the preliminary inquiry and what a witness has to say when he is giving evidence at the trial itself. I do not know whether David Gaunson had a copy of McIntyre's report, made to Pewtress, in which he makes the same sort of statement: 'Constable Lonigan made a motion toward the rifle which he was carrying.' This report was made even before he made the statement to Supt. Sadleir. I do not know whether Gaunson had a copy of the statement made to Supt. Sadleir; I doubt it. If it was so, it is another very unfortunate incident which occurred during this particular process.

That Const. McIntyre made previous inconsistent statements, and that he made them very shortly after the event, when it could be said that the events were vivid and burnt into his memory, should have been put to the jury. Those previous inconsistent statements should have been put fairly and squarely to him.

I think, without unfairness, that Bindon was very uncomfortable during his defence of Kelly. He was uncomfortable about putting self-defence fairly and squarely. He tried. He asked questions about Constable Fitzpatrick, particularly of Constable Day, the second witness.[1] It was clear then that Fitzpatrick was no longer a policeman and he asked Day why Fitzpatrick was no longer a policeman, but did not get anything from Day. It is again a pity he did not know that the incumbent Acting Commissioner of Police had scrawled across Constable Fitzpatrick's papers, right at the end, what the Royal Commission called 'this fine, valedictory memo', that he was 'a liar and a larrakin'.[2] He did not know, perhaps, that Constable Fitzpatrick had pleaded guilty on a number of occasions to serious disciplinary offences in the police, as he admitted to the Royal Commission in his evidence before it. He did not know that the Inspector-General of Police in N.S.W., where Fitzpatrick had come under notice on several occasions

[1] *Notes of Evidence,* p. 4.
[2] Royal Commission, 2nd Progress Report. *Parliamentary Papers of Legislative Assembly for 1881,* vol. III, p. x.

when he was on duty, had sent the most damning reports of him to his Victorian colleagues. All we can say, I think, is that perhaps if Molesworth had accepted the brief, if another fifty guineas had been obtained from the Crown, if a lot of 'ifs', then a different light might have been cast upon the matter. Then, possibly, there might have been a different verdict.

*Question:* It has been suggested that there might have been another trial judge other than Mr Justice Barry. How many Supreme Court judges were there on the Victorian Bench at the time?

*Waller:* There were five, the Chief Justice and four puisne justices.[3] But the work in those days, as today, was traditionally allocated by the Chief Justice. It is not a question of the Crown appointing a judge to try a particular case. The Chief Justice, in consultation no doubt with his other brethren, appoints judges to carry out the various duties that the court undertakes. There is nothing to suggest that there was anything curious about the appointment of Sir Redmond Barry to preside in the Central Criminal Court in Melbourne during October.

*J. Arrowsmith* (The *Tribune*): You referred to a process of law which had to be changed in 1878. To what process were you referring?

*Waller:* I was referring to the passage of the extraordinary statute called the *Felons Apprehension Act* 1878, (42 Vict., No. 612), which passed both Houses of the Victorian Parliament and was proclaimed in one single day, 1 November 1878. This Act was copied from a statute enacted in New South Wales in 1865 (28 Vict. No. 2) by a Legislature panic-stricken by the depredations of bushrangers.[4]

The Act provided for special proceedings to be taken

---

[3] Sir William Foster Stawell, Knt., Chief Justice; Sir Redmond Barry, Knt.; Robert Molesworth, Esq; James Wilberforce Stephen, Esq; George Higinbotham, Esq. The order is by date of appointment. Sir Redmond Barry was the senior puisne judge: see (1880) 6 V.L.R. *memoranda*, where his death on 23 November 1880 is recorded.

[4] The N.S.W. legislation of 1865 was continued by a statute enacted in 1879 (42 Vict. Nos. 9 and 13).

before a justice of the Supreme Court, at the instance of the Attorney-General, against any person charged with a capital crime. If this justice was satisfied that the accused was at large and would 'probably resist all attempts by the ordinary legal means of apprehending him', then he might issue a warrant for the apprehension of the accused requiring him to surrender himself for trial on a named date, the warrant to be published in the government *Gazette* and in such other place and papers best calculated to bring it to the accused's knowledge. The Act then went on to provide that if he did not surrender himself accordingly, the accused might be adjudged and declared to be an outlaw, such adjudication to be published in the *Gazette* and in one or more Melbourne and country newspapers. The Act went on as follows:

> If . . . such outlaw shall afterwards be found at large armed or there being reasonable ground to believe that he is armed it shall be lawful for any of Her Majesty's subjects whether a constable or not and without being accountable for the use of any deadly weapon in aid of such apprehension whether its use is preceded by a demand for surrender or not to apprehend or take such outlaw alive or dead.

*Keith Dunstan* (Melbourne *Sun*): Can you give me some facts about the Gaunson who defended Kelly?
*Waller:* David Gaunson was Kelly's attorney or solicitor. He appeared for him at the preliminary inquiry at Beechworth and instructed Bindon, the barrister who was Kelly's advocate at his trial. He was a member of the Legislative Assembly and also a Chairman of Committees. He became the object of a good deal of newspaper criticism, some of it quite vicious, because of his activities after Kelly's conviction. He was one of the leading spirits, together with his younger brother William and Hamilton, the Chairman of the Society for the Abolition of Capital Punishment, in

trying to rally public support in seeking a reprieve for Kelly. Their efforts in one sense were spectacularly successful. They called a meeting which 4,000 people attended at the *Hippodrome* in Melbourne, and that meeting unanimously endorsed a petition seeking mercy for Kelly. They managed to present a petition, with some 32,000 signatures gathered in a few days, to the Governor.

Afterwards the whole wrath of the newspaper establishment of the day fell upon Gaunson. There were very strong suggestions in papers throughout Victoria that the Legislative Assembly should take proceedings against him because, it was said, he had disgraced his high office as a Chairman of Committees by continuing with what was described as 'unseemly' (I think that was the most gentle word used) agitation after the verdict of guilty had been pronounced.

*Question:* Was it unreasonable at the time to refuse postponement of the trial for the reasons given?

*Waller:* This is a hard question to answer. It is always a matter in the discretion of the judge to whom the application has been made whether or not an adjournment is granted. The point that was taken by Smyth, the Crown Prosecutor, in opposing the adjournment was not an insubstantial one.

Smyth said that it had already been sworn in an affidavit made on 15 October that Gaunson, acting for Kelly, had known since 25 August that the trial was set down for the October sittings. Furthermore Gaunson was furnished with a copy of the depositions on 8 August. This is the sort of thing that would lead the trial judge to conclude that there was no surprise, in the sense that the defendant had not had time to prepare himself. This would make it, I think, entirely proper for him to say no.

In fact, there was an adjournment for ten days. Smyth finally said that he would not object to a couple of days' adjournment 'to show there is complete fairness to the prisoner', whereupon Barry stated that he would not be free until 28 October.

*Question:* Was it not possible that the defence wanted the extra time to allow the Government processes to go through to get the extra grant to obtain Molesworth?

*Waller:* That was another reason why the application was made. The Crown Law Department, through the Sheriff, had said the decision had been made. Gaunson was to undertake the defence on the usual conditions: 7 guineas for the attorney, plus 7 guineas for counsel and 5 shillings for his clerk. Then the Crown would consider, according to the length and complexity of the case, whether any further grant should be made. I have not been able completely to discover why those circumstances made it impossible to brief Molesworth, the barrister whose name was mentioned in those applications by Gaunson.

*Keith Dunstan:* What about the duration of the trial? Was it a track record? [*Laughter.*]

*Waller:* No. By today's standards it seems brief indeed. By the standards of the nineteenth century, particularly of the early nineteenth century, it was a lengthy trial. There are some instances recorded earlier in the nineteenth century of persons being arraigned, convicted and sentenced within the space of about a quarter of an hour.

In that light, it was no track record.

We have to remember when comparing trials then and today that some substantial changes have occurred in the criminal process in this State. There is the statute which permits the accused to give sworn evidence. There are other changes which have encouraged the accused to call evidence on his own behalf, and this leads to a lengthening of the process. If you talk today, for example, to the people in the Crown Law Department in Melbourne, they will tell you that criminal trials in 1967 tend to be longer than they were about ten years ago. This is explained, *inter alia,* by the fact that more accused men are represented by counsel.

*Question:* Why would the Crown hesitate in allowing the defence, in this case, sufficient funds to brief a man like Molesworth?

*Waller:* I don't know. Probably it was adherence to an

147

established practice. It could have been said — in fact it was said in so many words — with complete propriety, 'These are our usual terms'. This was an act of grace, after all. The Crown didn't have to pay. 'Our usual terms are 7 guineas for attorney, 7 guineas for counsel and 5 shillings for his clerk and that is what we grant him here. If it turns out that the trial is lengthy and very complex then we will entertain favourably an application for an additional amount.'

*Question:* When Kelly was talking to the judge, he said publicly that his counsel wasn't as well up on the facts as he was. Is that correct?

*Waller:* Yes. He said 'Mr Bindon knows nothing of my case and Mr Gaunson knows nothing either.'

*Question:* Did he then have confidence in his defence counsel?

*Waller:* There is one incident which indicates that on the second day of the trial he did not. One of the newspapers reported that it was pretty clear that Kelly wanted his counsel to sit down and he wanted to take over the cross-examination of the Crown witnesses himself. He was persuaded by Gaunson, with whom he was evidently conferring from time to time, not to do this, but to leave the matter in the hands of counsel. That incident, coupled with his later remarks in his colloquy with Sir Redmond Barry, indicates that, as the trial wore on, he must have become increasingly despondent about his counsel's capacity to make out his defence.

*Question:* Then why didn't Kelly defend himself? If he had increasingly less confidence in his counsel why did he not take over the questioning himself? Or why did he not tell the true and full story to his counsel prior to the preliminary trial at Beechworth.

*Waller:* One assumes that he *had*. I assume that he had told the story to Gaunson, who appeared for him at the preliminary inquiry at Beechworth, that they had interviews, that Gaunson knew what Kelly's story was.

*P. Beazley:* I believe that Sir Redmond Barry in fact presided at the trial of Mrs Kelly. I believe (this is only what I have read second-hand) that during the course of that trial, he said to Mrs Kelly, 'If your son was here, I would give him fifteen years.'

Now if he said that, would you think that it was proper of him to have accepted an appointment as presiding judge at Kelly's own trial?

Secondly (and this question is perhaps not answerable), in view of the comments Barry made at the end of the case and the conversation he had with Kelly, it seems apparent that he did not like him very much. He certainly had views about what he had done and whether he was a good man and so forth. Do you see any significance in the fact that twice during that conversation Kelly made rather interesting prophecies? First, when Barry pronounced the death sentence, he said, 'May the Lord have mercy on your soul.' Kelly said, 'Yes I will see you there.' Second, the reference to the higher court he would come to. Do you see any significance in the fact that a fortnight or so after Kelly was hanged, Sir Redmond Barry died rather suddenly? [*Laughter.*]

*Waller:* Well, that last story is quite fascinating, but I think that it is a story to be left to the Irish experts. [*laughter.*] It must have frightened the wits out of some people in Melbourne. As far as the first question you ask is concerned, I have heard the story about Barry's remarks at the trial of Mrs Kelly, Skillion and Williamson in respect of their aiding and abetting Ned Kelly in wounding Constable Fitzpatrick with intent to murder him. I don't know whether it ever happened, or is a bit of myth.

I think that a judge, having delivered himself of that kind of remark about a man who was now presented for trial on another, much more serious charge which had some connection with the matter in which he had made these remarks, should have recused himself. He should have said, 'I'm not going to sit on this particular trial. Let someone else who is not affected in this particular way sit.' But he did not, and no application was made to ask him to remove himself, either, as far as I can see. The story is probably apocryphal.

*Ian Jones:* On this point, I don't know of anyone else succeeding in finding the source of that alleged remark of Sir Redmond Barry's. It doesn't appear in any reports of the trial.

*Waller:* I read it in some book about the Kellys.

*Ian Jones:* There is no source for that remark that I can see. I am sure had the remark been made it would have been swooped on by reporters present who were particularly anti-Kelly in the course of this trial and in the course of the horse-stealing trial.

*Waller:* It is apparently without real foundation.

*Question:* In the application of the law in the matter of Lonigan in 1880, as you have put it, it looks very unsatisfactory. What would be the prospects of re-opening the case and giving some measure of reinstatement to relatives of Kelly? I suggest this because there is a rumour going around that there could be a re-opening of the Kelly case and a retired Supreme Court judge would do the job.

*Waller:* We have had a recent instance of what you describe as a re-opening. Nearly twelve months ago, Mr Justice Brabin, of the High Court of Justice in England, sat as a Committee to inquire into the case of Timothy John Evans, executed for murder in 1950.[5] That judge conducted, admittedly after a much shorter lapse of time than has occurred in our case, the kind of investigation to which you now allude. His 'verdict,' arrived at on a balance of probabilities, resulted in the issue of a posthumous pardon to Timothy John Evans. As a legal proposition it is entirely feasible. The question is whether there is sufficient basis to institute that kind of inquiry.

In respect of Timothy John Evans, of course, the worrying feature was not a defence that had not been properly put, or put at all. There the chief Crown witness against Evans was John Christie, a man who was afterwards con-

[5] Cmmd. 3101, 1966.

victed as a depraved murderer himself. It was 'factual difficulty', if you like, which arose for close examination only after there had been a final and complete disposition of Evans.

There are a couple of 'factual difficulties' here. There is the Fitzpatrick business, of course. It would be very difficult today to come to a firm conclusion (though we may have, I think, some strong beliefs), in the legal context, that Fitzpatrick was telling a pack of lies. The evidence seems to point that way. There is evidence about his own character, there is the internal evidence in the story of the shooting with the pistol in those confined circumstances, and there is 'the very minor wound' that the doctor said he found when he examined his arm. And then there is the evidence of McIntyre about what Lonigan actually did.

But you ask me if it is *possible*. The answer is that there *could* be an inquiry. There could be a complete re-sifting, made with very great difficulty, because of the very long lapse of time and the death, to my knowledge, of everyone who was actually connected with the matter. But there *could* be the same kind of result that was produced in the Evans case. I don't think that there is the necessary gunpowder to be lit under the executive government to move it to appoint a Royal Commission. In the Evans case, there was an enormous and consistently maintained pressure by many people both in Parliament and outside, which led to several inquiries.

*Question:* What was the record of the existing Government of the time in the carrying out and enforcing of the laws? We have been reminded continually during this School of Kelly's anathema to the police.

It has been said that Kelly believed the police at Stringybark Creek would destroy him rather than take him alive. This amounts almost to a feeling in Kelly's mind that the police had a vendetta against him. Now it has been stated during this School, that this, to a large extent, was due to his Irish heritage and the harsh measures imposed by the United Kingdom government on the people of Ireland in

151

the area where his father came from, that this was a family tradition. Kelly's father came from Tipperary in 1842; his mother came from County Down, which was not quite so depressed an area as Tipperary. But I have yet to hear anybody say what Kelly thought of himself as an Australian.

Kelly was an Australian by birth. The citizens whom he terrorized were Australian. Surely, when all is said and done, he was defying the laws of Australia, not the laws of Great Britain. There were many thousands of people who migrated to this country from Ireland, Scotland, from England itself, who adapted themselves to these conditions, which we would not tolerate today. They came out and tried to establish law and order and prosperity in this country and not anarchy, which we would have had if people like Kelly had been allowed to rule.

*Waller:* I do not know if I can say much in response to all those remarks. But let me say this. I have been concerned with Kelly's trial on a particular charge, *not* with his behaviour at Euroa and Jerilderie and at Glenrowan, and not, as I have tried to emphasize, with his killing of Constable Scanlon and Sergeant Kennedy later on that day in the Wombat Ranges.

One of the most significant of the imports into this country, a vital part of the English heritage, was the already developed system of English criminal law. A most important aspect of that system is that a man is entitled to a fair trial, and to a fair defence, in respect of *the particular charge* which is presently levelled against him. Now you may charge a man, in respect of the same incident, with a large number of crimes. It is proper if he is given a fair trial in respect of each one.

The points that I have tried to make have been in the context of that one trial for the murder of Constable Lonigan. It is that crime of which Kelly was found guilty. He was never tried for any other crimes.

Let me point out again that one cannot say with absolute certainty that the verdict in this case was a verdict which would not have been arrived at by the jury had they heard the case presented in the way in which I have tried to put it. As to that, all I say is that there is a *possibility* that they might have decided to bring in a verdict of manslaughter, the verdict that Barry said was not open to them. It would then have been open to the Crown to proceed with the presentment in respect of Constable Scanlon, when it might have been very much harder for Kelly to say that he had behaved in a reasonable manner. He had time to ride away, to escape, having discovered from McIntyre where the other men had gone.

The Crown might then have proceeded with an information charging Kelly with the wilful murder of Sergeant Kennedy. It would have been entirely proper to have tried every single charge that could be laid against Kelly.

I have only been concerned with one.

## 6

# A New View of Ned Kelly

IAN JONES

I almost feel like echoing Ned Kelly's words at his trial: 'It is rather late for me to speak now.'

I feel particular humility following so closely on Professor Waller's brilliant discussion of Ned Kelly's trial. However, perhaps it is appropriate that we should follow an examination of a legal judgment on Ned Kelly with what amounts to a moral judgment. Ned Kelly was found guilty, legally.

Was he guilty morally?

What I shall attempt is to look very quickly at some important aspects of the man which perhaps we have not glimpsed yet; to look at the conditions which led up to Ned Kelly's personal revolt against injustice; to look at the conditions in the north-eastern district and in Victoria as a whole, which created a situation in which rebellion could develop. We shall look at the way in which Kelly's personal rebellion became associated with a broader rebellion of the selector class in the north-east, centred on the Irish-Australians of the immediate Kelly country. We shall see how Kelly eventually rejected the support of these people in his personal rebellion — the greatest moral judgment of his life — and how, at the end, the rebellion of these selectors was resolved, more than a year after the destruction of the Kelly gang.

Looking for a symbol of Ned Kelly one inevitably starts with something like the Nolan pictures. They are tremendously exciting, and they have a great validity. Here we have a beautiful interpretation of the land — a super-realistic impression of the Kelly country and Australia as a whole. And superimposed are these naïve, almost child-like figures. It is as though these are memories of childhood tales viewed against the country as we know it today; and most unrealistic of all is the figure of Ned Kelly himself, a dark and forbidding figure, almost like some inter-planetary visitor — a symbol of cosmic justice, who is striding the earth for a time to strike down these universal and timeless figures of authority and oppression which throng around him.

The armour has become Ned Kelly's symbol, but it has also become the great bar between us and an understanding of the man. Even though we have now seen several photographs of Ned Kelly, he still remains a faceless, in-human figure. He is almost anonymous behind the plough-steel helmet. We must strip this away before we can even see the man, and then we have to find out what was going on in his mind. The task is an enormous one.

First, very quickly, take off the armour and what do you find? You find a man just under six feet, a man of in-credible physical impact. And this is the thing that strikes you about Kelly, the enormous impact of the man on everyone he met. Whether the impression was good or bad, hostile or sympathetic, the impact was there. Physically, Ned Kelly was almost superhuman. This sounds an ex-travagant statement in every way, but the man *was* physi-cally remarkable. He was an outstanding boxer, who in his twentieth year became regarded as an unofficial heavy-weight boxing champion of the north-east. He gained this recognition by defeating 'Wild' Wright in a fantastic twenty-round bare-knuckle fight. Wright was six foot two and thirteen stone and fought like a threshing machine. One old man described him to me as 'a great bony man with a great bony face, a black moustache, and the fiercest pair of eyes you would ever see'. Another said, 'mad as a tiger snake that had been run over by a mob of sheep'. Ned Kelly's boxing prowess was symptomatic of strength and endurance which he displayed to a spectacular degree in his Last Stand.

Ned Kelly was a crack horseman, but not, we are told, a highly polished horseman. He lacked the finesse of Tom Lloyd or Steve Hart but, in a district of horsemen, in a colony of horsemen, in a country of horsemen, Ned Kelly was acknowledged to be one of the finest trick riders that the people of his time had seen. He was also a crack shot. He had a set of qualities which would make him attractive to the people of this time and place. Yet despite the talk of his being a bully and a braggart, he emerges as a surprisingly quiet and gentle man. Throughout his life and outlawry there were dozens of touches showing this gentle side of Ned Kelly. My friend and colleague, Keith McMenomy, has done extensive research on the boyhood of Ned Kelly and finds constant reference to his being a 'quiet' lad.

Far from urging the gang on to further excesses, Ned Kelly emerges as a restraining figure, a man curbing the hotheads among the sympathizers. A man saying: 'We are not going to massacre police, we are not going to hold up banks holusbolus'. Yet, he was a man who, when it was roused, had tremendous anger.

He possessed a degree of vanity, but not without some reason. He was justly proud of his boxing ability. He dressed well — he was proud of his personal appearance.

Of all his characteristics, the one that probably brought about his downfall more than any other was that he trusted people — and this is a good measure of a man. A man who trusts people is usually himself reliable. Ned Kelly trusted Fitzpatrick to an almost ludicrous degree, and, of course, he trusted Curnow.

Ned Kelly was utterly devoted to his family. He committed the unforgivable sin of being devoted to his mother. He does not speak much of his father, certainly. His father died when he was eleven, let us not forget. But all the indications are that both Ned and his mother were proud of 'Red' Kelly, and at his first bushranging act, Ned Kelly proudly declared: 'I am Ned Kelly, son of Red Kelly, and a finer man never put his feet in two shoes'. He was devoted to his sisters, and also, in his way, to his brother Dan.

All evidence points to the fact that Ned and Dan did not get on well together. This was probably not Ned's fault. It seems that Dan bitterly resented the dominant place of Ned in the Kelly family. He resented the fact that Ned Kelly, since the age of eleven or so, had been a father to the family; but more than this, that Ned was physically big. Jim was even bigger than Ned, and poor young Dan, the youngest son, indulged and spoilt by the mother who had lost her husband, had to wear his brothers' cast-off clothes, and had the humiliation of being photographed in coats with turned-up sleeves and pants with turned-up cuffs. At Stringybark Creek, even, Constable McIntyre remarked that Dan Kelly's clothes were so big that when viewed from the back, the boy inside them could hardly be seen. But despite the resentment, the over-assertion of Dan, Ned Kelly patiently continued his father role and tried to keep the hot-headed boy out of trouble.

Over many of Ned Kelly's actions we see this paternalism. Look at a photo of him taken about 1875; the impression is of a man of years — a man of substance, the father of many children. It is difficult to believe he is a lad of twenty-one, with his spade beard, his proud, rather benign face, his slightly old-fashioned but thoroughly good clothes. Kelly carried his paternalism into much of what he did — into his very conduct of the Kelly outbreak.

Finally, in this very hurried and necessarily rather superficial look at some qualities of the man, I must reiterate what has already been said. What you have heard illustrated from the Jerilderie Letter, what you heard expounded so vividly by Professor Manning Clark: the fact that Ned Kelly was Irish.

Two hundred years or more of bitterness and hatred lay behind him. He was the son of an Irish convict, inextricably involved with a clan of wild Irishmen who, deservedly or not, were in constant trouble with the police.

The story of Ned Kelly's personal rebellion against what amounted to police persecution of the Kelly family has been told many times. It has been told in, I think, an extreme form in Kenneally's *Complete Inner History of the Kelly Gang and Their Pursuers.* This was the first statement of the thesis in any coherent way and Kenneally perhaps went too far. He was too strident. The 'persecution' thesis has been restated, rather uncritically, by Max Brown, and by Frank Clune.

Perhaps the statement still remains a little extreme, but the fact remains that the Kelly family were persecuted, to a degree, by the police. We have the famous, much-quoted, but inescapable report sent by Superintendent Nicholson to Captain Standish in 1877.[1]

> I visited the notorious Mrs Kelly's house on the road from hence [Wangaratta] to Benalla. She lived on a piece of cleared and partially cultivated land on the roadside, in an old wooden hut with a large bark roof. The dwelling was divided into five apartments, by partitions of blanketing, rugs etc. There were no men in the house, only children and two girls of about fourteen years of age, said to be her daughters. [Superintendent Nicholson would have nothing put over him!] They all appeared to be existing in poverty and squalor. She said her sons were out at work but did not indicate where, and that their relatives seldom came near them. However, their communications with each other are known to the police. [There had to be underground communication between Mrs Kelly and her sisters and brothers-in-law.] Until the gang referred to is rooted out of the neighbourhood, one of the most experienced and successful mounted constables in the district will be required in charge of Greta.

Then the instruction that went out: 'Without oppressing the people or worrying them in any way you should en-

[1] Royal Commission. Q.1024 *et seq.*

158

deavour, whenever they commit any paltry crime, to bring them to justice and send them to Pentridge. Even on a paltry sentence.'

Although this report dates from Ned Kelly's twenty-third year, it accurately depicts the background against which he grew to manhood. Ned Kelly was a juvenile delinquent. Let us not avoid that fact. And let us not forget that in this period, Ned Kelly was given a fair deal by the police. In his first major brush with the law, he was charged as an accomplice of the bushranger Harry Power. He received a fair trial and was acquitted. There is no doubt that Kelly was helping Harry Power. However, at the trial identification was inconclusive and he was acquitted. The police were particularly impressed with young Kelly. They thought he showed great potential. Superintendent Nicholson began to make arrangements for Ned Kelly to be sent up to a station in New South Wales. Nothing came of this.

By the time he was nineteen, Ned Kelly had served three years' hard labour for receiving a stolen horse. But he came out of prison determined to try to lead an honest life. As I see it, Kelly had been greatly influenced by the Pentridge Chaplain, Father O'Hea, who, six years later, stood beside him on the scaffold in his last moments of life. Tradition has it that Father O'Hea had baptized Ned Kelly. We have managed to locate records showing the baptism of Jim and Margaret Kelly by Father O'Hea.[2] In the eyes of the Church, I am told, this provides the moral certitude of Ned Kelly's baptism, and a good indication that the baptism had been performed by Father O'Hea.

With these facts established, it is not difficult to imagine that it was Father O'Hea who persuaded Ned to try to lead an honest life when he left prison.

For nearly three years, Ned Kelly did just this, and these were important years. In this time Ned Kelly worked as a faller for two timber mills. He had his famous boxing match. He set up as a building contractor and worked with granite, which he had apparently learnt to quarry and

[2] Baptism Records, St. Paul's, Coburg.

159

handle in the Beechworth Gaol. There is a granite home still standing in the Winton district which was built by Ned Kelly and his brothers.[3] There are also several barns and sheds around the Kelly country which, local tradition attests, were built by the Kelly boys. Sometimes Ned worked as a shearer. He became the district's leading trick horseman and was a popular figure at the impromptu rodeos which local lads used to stage from time to time.

Eventually, one of the firms that had employed him as a faller took over a sawmill in his home town. They had been so impressed with young Kelly that they hired him as overseer of the mill.

Ned Kelly abandoned his honest life through a trifling incident which he describes in the Jerilderie Letter. He ran in a wild bull and gave it to a man who sold it. A squatter is supposed to have claimed that the bull had been stolen from him. Ned Kelly confronted him. The squatter, James Whitty, is said to have backed down before witnesses, and admitted that in fact the bull was not his. Whatever the truth of the story, Ned Kelly had made a dangerous enemy, and he had also landed in the middle of a bitter land war being waged between Whitty and other squatters of the district, and the small selectors. Many of these were Irish-Australians, battling to make a living in times which were, at the best, tough, and which were being aggravated by bad seasons and deteriorating economic conditions.

We come towards the Fitzpatrick incident. This occurred in the autumn of 1878.

It is almost a truism to say that the Kelly outbreak had its roots in the social and economic patterns of the 1870s. Now, what were these patterns and how did they interlock with the genesis of The Trouble? How did they interlock with James Whitty and his enmity for Ned Kelly? And with Fitzpatrick and his attempt to arrest Dan Kelly in those mysterious events of 15 April at the Kelly homestead?

In the late 1870s, there was a series of bad seasons in

[3] 'A True Story of the Kelly Gang.' Unpublished MS by Joseph Ashmead, a contemporary and friend of the Kelly family.

Victoria. The gold yield had been falling every year. There was an economic depression and acute political ferment. Drought and grasshopper plagues aggravated the land war between the squatters and the selectors.

A man like Ned Kelly, who was a potential leader of the selectors — a figurehead — appeared all the more dangerous in a period like this. Opposition of a man like Ned Kelly, leading and uniting selectors in their battle against the squatters, could not be tolerated. At the same time the Upper and Lower Houses of Victoria were locked in a life and death struggle over the purse-strings of Government, which was brought to a crisis by the huge cost of supposedly adequately fortifying the colony against a feared Russian invasion. Directly, this led to the notorious Black Wednesday of 8 January 1878, which saw the wholesale sacking of civil servants, including county court justices and police magistrates. This was a desperate means to eke out the dwindling finance of Government as expenditure drained the last supply vote. Disbandment of the police department was initiated. Eventually this measure was abandoned, but police expenditure was hacked back. Men who left the force were not replaced, and many country stations were broken up.[4]

Any constable remotely unsure of his position at such a time would understandably try to convince his superiors of his zeal and his value to the force. Just as Constable Fitzpatrick did, first in trying to have Ned Kelly arrested in Benalla for drunkenness, and second, in going out of his way to arrest Dan Kelly. Once and for all, he was trying to prove that — far from being an intimate of the Kelly circle, a possible boy-friend of Kate Kelly, and a mate of Ned Kelly's — he was in fact, a redoubtable foe of the Kellys and a valued man to have in the district.

This was a demoralized community. It was a period of bad debts and bankruptcy in all levels of society. People

[4] The effect of Black Wednesday on the Force is discussed by Sadleir, J., in his *Recollections of a Victorian Police Officer* (Melbourne, 1913).

161

in almost every town could see bank managers and officers being charged with embezzling funds, the town clerk or shire secretary absconding with public money. There were bank failures, mass meetings of unemployed.

The Premier was soon to speak of 'broken heads and houses in flames'. He was being accused of trading on class bitterness, utilizing to his own advantage 'the differences between capital and labour introduced by the old squat-tocracy'.[5] Victoria was ready for rebellion. And within the already explosive bounds of Victoria as a whole were the smaller, more tightly knit, and even more potentially explosive groups of Irish-Australian selectors.[6]

Mr Bate brilliantly portrayed the plight of the selector in this period. Add to this the feeling of the Irish-Aus-tralians, people with a legacy of bitterness against British rule, many of whom had been transported, or whose fathers, uncles, or brothers had suffered transportation. Many had deserted Ireland — if that is a fair word — during those terrible years of what we call the Potato Famine and what Irishmen still regard as the punitive starvation of a people by their rulers.

The enemies of these people were, inevitably, the large landholders — men of money and influence; and just as inevitably, the police allegiance lay with the squatters, be-cause of their money and their political influence.

Among the police, who would be more hated by the Irish-Australian selector than the Irishmen who had 'de-serted the shamrock, the ash corner, the emblem of all true beauty',[7] as Ned said, and had put on the hated 'jacket';

[5] *Ovens and Murray Advertiser*, 8 August 1878.

[6] The picture of the late 1870s given in this paper is questioned in the discussion that follows. Because of the importance of this picture to the entire thesis, I should reiterate that, while conscious of my position as an amateur historian among justly respected professionals, I can find no reason to alter my views, which are based entirely on primary material. They represent a concentrated study of metro-politan and provincial papers and periodicals from 1875 to 1881— chief among them the *Argus*, the *Australasian Sketcher* and the *Ovens and Murray Advertiser*.

[7] Jerilderie Letter.

162

the man who had his ammunition pouch thrown across his shoulder with the symbol of Victoria Regina emblazoned on it in nickel for everyone to see, who strode through the dusty streets of little towns in his highly polished jack boots, with his spurs and his splendid black military-looking helmet?

The Irishman in this uniform was a hated figure. Police alliance with the squatters alienated them from selectors, as a class. But the antagonism of Irish selectors to Irish policemen reached a level that might best be described as religious war.

We have seen in earlier discussions that the situation in the north-east was being recognized by the authorities. We have already seen the recognized threat implicit in the particularly heavy calendar facing the Spring Assizes at Beechworth in 1878. We have noted the harsh sentences delivered against Mrs Kelly and Skillion and Williamson in the Fitzpatrick Trial as being merely symptomatic of the severity of the sentences handed out by Sir Redmond Barry against all the prisoners convicted at this historic Assize. Barry, for the time, became a hated figure — a sort of Cromwell of the 1870s — because Redmond Barry, a great man of the colony, a senior Judge of the British Empire, was also an Irishman.

Now, into this tinderbox of discontent and potential rebellion dropped the Stringybark Creek gun fight. Three policemen — three Irishmen — were killed by Ned and Dan Kelly, and two men who, for the moment, were unknown.

And the word was abroad. Ned Kelly's mother was sentenced to three years' imprisonment on 12 October. Two weeks later, three police died at the hands of Mrs Kelly's son.

We are tempted to say that the fuse of rebellion was lit and that the people of the north-east recognized Ned Kelly as their champion. But this is not quite true. There was no immediate support for the Kellys from any but their close friends and relatives. In fact, the first reaction to

Stringybark Creek was one of horror and panic. Selectors feared a return to the black days of bushranging, the anarchy of the gold rush period — pillage, rape, murder. Bullockies and teamsters camped by the roadside or travelled in convoys, too frightened to travel alone.

The fear, the suspicion of the Kellys, is readily understandable. It is still easy to interpret Stringybark Creek as the act of a gang of bushrangers making their first blow against the police. In point of fact, Stringybark Creek was an act of personal rebellion by Ned Kelly. A personal blow against police who had come out after him and his brother, an act in which Joe Byrne and Steve Hart happened to be implicated. Any two, three, four, out of a dozen men could have been with Ned and Dan Kelly at their hut on Bullock Creek the day Lonigan, Kennedy, Scanlon and McIntyre came to camp at nearby Stringybark Creek. It just happened to be Joe Byrne and Steve Hart.

So this ghastly fracas took place. Three men were dead, one man had escaped. And suddenly these four boys were outside the law. Ned Kelly regarded himself as responsible for this and, with what I can only describe as paternalism, regarded it as his responsibility now to look after three young men in the best way he could.

They were fugitives, soon to be outlawed. They had to live. Led by Ned Kelly, they conducted two brilliantly planned and executed bank robberies, probably the two most immaculate exploits in the history of Australian bushranging. There was hardly a hint of violence or offence in either. Suddenly people began to see a paradox in these exploits. Four young desperadoes viciously murder three troopers. Then suddenly the group emerges as a band of gentlemen bushrangers, holding up a squatter's homestead, treating the women courteously, holding hostages overnight, treating them well; with Ned Kelly himself spending the greater part of the night with his prisoners, speaking to them at length about the injustice and persecution levelled against his family.

Then came an even more confident blow at Jerilderie —

with its magnificent flair and its many wonderful touches. Bailing up the police, putting them in their own cells, donning their uniforms, taking the Senior Constable's wife across to decorate the courthouse for the Church service, having their horses shod and charging it to the New South Wales Government, Joe Byrne masquerading as a drunk to get from the Royal Mail Hotel to the Bank of New South Wales next door, the manager being surprised in his bath, and Ned Kelly's long speech to the bar-full of not-too-unhappy prisoners: all this suddenly gave people a new view of the Stringybark Creek murderers.

At Ned Kelly's trial, four people who had been involved in these holdups — four Crown witnesses — rather embarrassed the Prosecution by offering character references for Ned Kelly. Four of them pointed out that in Ned Kelly's account of the killings at Stringybark Creek, he was going out of his way to incriminate himself to protect the others. Mr Scott, manager of the bank at Euroa, went even further, and hastened to point out how courteous and gentlemanly Mr Kelly had been to himself and his wife. The Crown Prosecutor snapped: 'And he then robbed the Bank of £2,000. I suppose that is being gentlemanly and courteous?'[8] A garrison artilleryman who arrived at Euroa soon after the robbery encountered many people who already saw the Kellys as 'police-made criminals'.

But even before Jerilderie, the authorities themselves had swung a huge body of people throughout the north-east toward support of the gang. On 4 January 1879, the first of the Kelly sympathizers were arrested — twenty-one of them initially — and lodged in the Beechworth Gaol. For more than three months these people were remanded from week to week. They did not face trial. Week by week, some were released, others arrested. By 22 April, there were still thirteen men in custody. On that date they were released, still without being tried. The injustice of this stupid maneouvre was aggravated by the fact that the period of the sympathizers' imprisonment straddled the harvest time. We would

[8] 'The Trial of Ned Kelly'. Unpublished MS by Robin Corfield.

have to analyse very closely the conduct of every one of these men before the Kelly outbreak to find out the full story. We know some of the stories, however, and one in particular.

Jack McMonigle's great sin was that he had been Ned Kelly's leading hand at the Burke's Hole farm sawmill, where Kelly had been overseer. If one can believe the traditions of the McMonigle family, Jack McMonigle had gone to the Kelly family shortly after Stringybark Creek and asked that Ned should not call to see him. Jack McMonigle did not hold with murder, and if the police came to ask him if he had seen Ned Kelly he wanted to be able to tell the truth. Jack McMonigle was arrested as a Kelly sympathizer. He knew his crops were growing rank as the time of the harvest was passing, and it was Jack McMonigle who said: 'If the police don't let us out soon, they are going to have more than the Kelly gang to fight'. If the story is apocryphal, it was believed by people who knew McMonigle. And it was one of many such stories.[9] Superintendent Hare admitted: 'The police . . . had no evidence against these persons beyond the fact that they were known to be associates, relatives, and friends of the outlaws.[10]

One way or another, the sympathizers' harvests were brought in. It was another bad season and about a quarter of the harvest was destroyed by rust, anyway.

July of this year saw the Bank failures in Melbourne. Again this terrible discontent, this terrible ferment. People in the north-east were bitterly angry, resentful, worried about the future, the weather, the money they may or may not have had in the Bank. Worried about the banks themselves. And suddenly, in July, a little announcement in the *Mansfield Guardian* that selections were being refused to persons supposed to be sympathizers of the Kelly gang. Typical was the case of Bill Tanner — a prominent sympathizer. Refused a selection in the Myrrhee district, he

[9] Ashmead, *op. cit.*

[10] Superintendent Hare, *The Last of the Bushrangers* (London, 1895).

asked the reason and received the following reply from the Secretary for Lands:

'16th June 1879. To Mr William Tanner, Myrrhee. Sir, Referring to your letter of the 9th instant, enquiring the reason why your application for 44a or 4p, parishes of Myrrhee and Tatong, was refused, I have the honour to inform you that the land was refused on the recommendation of the Police Department.'[11]

At this period the land problems of Ireland in the 1840s were green memories. The Devon Land Commission in Ireland had been told that the Irish peasantry were usually good-humoured and kind, but that they became absolutely merciless where occupation of the land was in question. A witness said: 'I never knew them to attack anyone for money, but touch the farm and turn them out and they get frantic and wild.' The Commission subsequently said in its report: 'The one absorbing feeling as to the possession of land stifles all others and extinguishes the plainest principles of humanity.'[12]

In the colony of Victoria in 1879, the same instincts were stirred, and this, I believe, was the turning point in the support of the Kelly gang.

Many people had already committed themselves as sympathizers of the gang. Men were walking all over the north-east with their chinstraps under their noses, the badge of the Kelly sympathizer. (It had been the badge of the Greta mob, the bunch of young bucks Dan Kelly used to lead around the country. They had worn their chinstraps under their noses in an old goldfield fashion, much as Australian soldiers did in the Second World War.) Now the sympathizer with the hat band under his nose was a marked man who would not be allowed to hold land in the Kelly country. Ned had given much of the proceeds of the Jeril-

---

[11] Royal Commission, Q.3553.
[12] Cecil Woodham-Smith, *The Great Hunger* (London, 1962).

derie and Euroa robberies to friends and relatives throughout the north-east. Much of the Euroa money had been hard to trace; Euroa gold had been sold to Chinese goldbuyers and the proceeds distributed. The Jerilderie notes were more easily identifiable. And Bank of New South Wales notes, smelling of earth, had been passed all over the north-east, by people whose names had been noted.[13]

In the eyes of Ned Kelly, he now became responsible for the barring of these people from the means of earning their livelihood. His responsibility had grown. It was not just a family — or three young fugitives — whom he had to look after. Suddenly, there were hundreds of people who, because of him, were facing possible disaster. Already there had been hints of something bigger than a bank robbery from the Kelly gang. In the letter which he tried to get published at Jerilderie, Ned Kelly said:

It will pay the Government to give those people who are suffering in innocence, justice and liberty. If not I will be compelled to show some colonial strategem which will open the eyes not only of the Victoria police and its inhabitants but also the whole British army. And no doubt they will acknowledge that their hounds are barking at the wrong stump and that Fitzpatrick will be the cause of greater slaughter to the Union Jack than St Patrick was to the snakes and toads in Ireland.

'Some colonial strategem'? What did he mean by that? Was this just bravado? Was this the braggart, swaggering Ned Kelly, waving his revolver in the air and shouting, 'I'll show the beggars! I'll show them! I'll teach them!' Perhaps so. Not long after this, Joe Byrne's mother — poor little hard-working Margaret Byrne — initially ashamed and embarrassed by the fact that her son had become an outlaw, was heard to say: 'My son and his mates will shortly do

[13] The Kelly Papers contain dozens of police reports documenting the distribution of money from Euroa and Jerilderie.

something that will astonish not only Australia but the whole world'. Max Brown said: 'Like a fist flung up against the sky.' Was Mrs Byrne swaggering, blustering, waving her bony little hand for nothing? Was there really going to be 'a colonial strategem'? And if there was, what would it be?

From this period there dates the legend of the Republic of North-Eastern Victoria. Max Brown mentions it. I have heard the story from many different people, told usually as a deep and dark piece of information — once or twice referred to as the United States of Australia. Whether this was Ned Kelly's concept, Joe Byrne's concept; whether it had filtered through from the ideas of American Republicanism given to Ned Kelly by his American step-father, George King; whether it sprang from some politically-minded person among the sympathizers trying to realize, in this growing rebellion in the north-east, the great promise of Ned Kelly, the figurehead; whether Ned Kelly was trying to fuse this movement into a second Eureka Stockade, we will never know. We cannot get inside the mind of Ned Kelly to this extent. But the fact is indisputable that, by the beginning of 1880, the rebellion was taking shape.

Professor Manning Clark said that, at this period, the Kellys' money was dwindling and the numbers of the sympathizers were dwindling. This seems to have been an optimistic police view.

The indications are that there was still enough money and more than enough sympathizers.

In fact, in a famous communication from one of the police spies we have a clear evidence on this point. During January and February of 1880 there had been some mysterious thefts around the Greta district — mould-boards were disappearing from ploughs. Towards the end of May, a letter reached Superintendent Nicholson from an agent called Kennedy, who was called the 'diseased stock agent', because, in referring to the Kelly gang, he used the code phrase 'diseased stock'. He addressed Nicholson always as 'Mr William Charles Balfour' for some reason best known to himself. His letter ran:

> Greta, May, 20, 1880.
>
> Mr William Charles Balfour, Benalla,
> Dear Sir,
> Nothing definite re the diseased stock of this locality. I have made careful inspection but did find [sic] exact source of disease. I have seen and spoken to —— and —— on Tuesday who were fencing their home. [Probably Ned and Dan Kelly, who at this stage had been seen building a fence right beside Kelly's Gap Road at the Kelly homestead.] All others I have not been able to see. Missing portions of cultivators described as jackets are now being worked and fit splendidly. Tested previous to using and proof at ten yards.

He ended his letter with the cryptic little phrase: 'Other animals are, I fear, diseased.'

The Kelly 'disease' was spreading.[14]

The Kellys were making armour. What were they going to do with it? Were they making armour to rob banks? The events of the next couple of months may remain eternally a mystery unless we are prepared to accept the oral traditions of the men who were closest to Ned Kelly, Joe Byrne, Dan Kelly and Steve Hart during those months of autumn and early winter of 1880.

Linked with the legend of the Republic of North-East Victoria, we learn that Ned Kelly was forming a selector army. The plan was simple. The gang, with their armour, would act as the shock troopers — the tanks — of the army. They would give their best guns to the sympathizers. The Kellys, with their armour to protect them, would retain the obsolete guns they had acquired during their outlawry — the old sawn-off repeaters, the percussion pis-

[14] Royal Commission, Q.755.

tols, the unreliable Colt revolving rifle. The police Martini-Henry rifle with which they had tested the armour, Scanlon's Spencer repeating rifle, the Adams and Tranter revolvers and all their other modern arms would go to the sympathizers.

Suddenly, with a plan forming, the decision was reached to kill Aaron Sherritt. Then we have bait for the trap, and the plan is quite clear. Sherritt was to be killed at Beechworth. On receipt of the news, a special train would leave Melbourne and pick up at Benalla the major body of police and blacktrackers and horses. The force would travel to Wangaratta, and change trains for Beechworth. What more logical place to strike at the train than Glenrowan, between Benalla and Wangaratta, home town of the gang, the centre of their greatest support and strength, where their flanks were safest?

While Joe Byrne and Dan Kelly killed Sherritt, Ned Kelly and Steve Hart would occupy Glenrowan, gather hostages and break the railway line. After a few hours' wait, during which Joe and Dan would have reached Glenrowan, the train would climb through Glenrowan, gather speed around the bend, and crash over the embankment. In their armour, with their obsolete guns, the gang would move in and mop up the survivors. Two rockets, supplied by Chinese sympathizers, were then to be fired from McDonnell's Railway Tavern, the second Glenrowan inn, and from all over the Kelly country, the sympathizers would ride at the gallop, clutching the guns which had been given to them by the gang, to follow them in raids on the banks at Benalla, Wangaratta, possibly Beechworth. And then what? The Republic of Victoria? Holding the Governor to ransom? We don't know.

Probably very few of the sympathizers knew the full extent of the plan. Certainly, some of them believed that the plan was only to stop the police train, turn it around, and take it back to Melbourne as a bargaining point to gain the release of Mrs Kelly and to put forward the cause of the selectors, the Kelly family, and their friends. We know that the plan was to destroy the train. This was a ruthless and brutal act, but it wasn't a criminal act. This was an act of war. If we are making a moral judgement of Kelly, we have to look at his plan in this light. This was the act of the Maquis who blew up German troop trains and moved in with grenades and tommyguns to mop up the survivors, or who, when the Germans were fleeing from Paris, tossed Molotov cocktails into open troop trucks. Brutal and ruthless, but war!

We now know something of the plan behind the Glenrowan campaign. Why was it never put into operation? We know, to a point.

We know the incredible delay in the police train reaching Glenrowan. We have noted earlier, the decay in the gang. We have noted their foolish conduct at Glenrowan; but perhaps we forget that these men had been awake Saturday, all through Saturday night, all through Sunday and that it was now 2 a.m. on the Monday. Curnow stopped the police train. It moved into Glenrowan. The first volleys were exchanged. A sympathizer, whose name we know, was waiting at McDonnell's Railway Tavern to fire the two rockets (a big one and a small one) which would signal the sympathizers to gallop to Glenrowan. He panicked. The train had not been wrecked. But he could see that fighting had started. He fired the two signal rockets.[15]

From as far away as Stanley, the sympathizers started gathering. Lookouts had been waiting for the firing of the rockets and the word spread. They started galloping toward Glenrowan. Ned Kelly, too, had seen the rockets. Immediately, he left the hotel to meet the sympathizers.

There are confusing and conflicting accounts of the exact meeting-place. It was apparently somewhere around the shoulder of Mount Glenrowan, not far from where the tracks had been torn up to destroy the train. Ned — already wounded — met the sympathizers. A shot had pierced his left arm in two places, twice through the lower arm, twice through the upper arm. He had been wounded in the

[15] Royal Commission, Q.11, 190.

172

left foot. By some miracle, he had mounted the grey mare Music and met the sympathizers on horseback.

The eye-witness accounts of this extraordinary meeting are confused and contradictory. It was dark. Confusion reigned. They were in scrub. No one knew how many had gathered. One said 30, another 150. But, they were there with their guns. And Kelly was there, wounded. He spoke to them. There remain two fragments of what he said: 'This is our fight' and 'I am prepared to die'. Melodramatic, perhaps, but terribly important.[16]

At that stage, there were only about sixteen policemen attacking the Glenrowan Hotel. If there had been only twelve sympathizers, the gang would have been at least on equal terms with the police. But, in that moment, Ned Kelly made the moral judgement that, because the plan had miscarried and this would not be an easy victory, he could no longer involve these people (who had their own worries and fears for the future) in his personal rebellion. Kelly turned the sympathizers back, ordered them to take no part in the fight, and prepared to return to the inn. Tom Lloyd, his cousin, who was probably closer to Ned Kelly than any other human being, remained with him.

A little before five o'clock, Ned Kelly returned to the Glenrowan Inn. This seems unbelievable, but it is true. Verification can be found of this in several sources. Kelly was apparently inside the inn when Joe Byrne was shot, shortly after five o'clock,[17] and was seen leaving the inn by Constable Gascoigne who reported the fact to Superintendent Sadleir.[18]

Ned Kelly rejoined Tom Lloyd, apparently believing that Dan and Steve Hart were following him. In the con-

[16] Regrettably, it is impossible to identify the men who have provided accounts of Ned Kelly's meeting with the sympathizers. Several versions tally in essential detail, with each other and with the documentary evidence relating to this remarkable incident.

[17] Royal Commission, Q.9484 *et. seq.*

[18] Sadleir and Gascoigne both discuss this in their Royal Commission evidence. Sadleir reiterates the point in his *Recollections of a Victorian Police Officer.*

fusion, they were not. At about this stage, Kelly collapsed. He had been losing blood now for something like three hours. He revived and asked Tom Lloyd to bring him his revolving rifle, which he had dropped. When it was brought to him, he discovered that the nipples were clogged with blood from his wounds.[19]

So, as dawn broke through the gap, he armed himself with his three revolvers and prepared to make his last attempt at rescuing Dan Kelly and Steve Hart from the Glenrowan Inn. At full daylight, when the sun had actually risen, but before it was shining through the gap, he started his last, magnificent, possibly futile attempt to rescue from the police these two young men. There were now thirty-four policemen attacking the Glenrowan Inn. Ned Kelly had been losing blood for more than five hours in near-zero temperatures. He was carrying ninety-seven pounds of armour.

We know the story of the last stand. There was a gunfight of less than half an hour in which some seventeen shots hit Ned Kelly's armour and during which he suffered twenty-eight separate shot wounds. Deathly pale, drained of blood, exhausted, mauled by shot, bruised by the bullets that smashed into his helmet, he was stripped of his armour. His arms and legs were so mangled that he could not bear to be carried. He had to walk to the railway station with Dan, and, possibly, Steve Hart trying to pick him off on the way. They were not going to allow Ned to be caught.

In the opinion of his doctors, Ned Kelly had no will to live. But he was too tough to die. He would be nursed back to health, tried and executed.

This should have been the end of the story, but in many ways it was only the beginning. What of the men who were not allowed to hold land in the Kelly country? What of these men whom Ned Kelly had ordered to stay out of the fight? They waited around the outskirts of the siege while

[19] Oral traditions of the sympathizers are confirmed by a report from Sergeant Steele in the Kelly papers (dated 10 August 1880) in which he discusses Ned Kelly's movements before the Last Stand.

Ned Kelly was captured. They were seen by several police, waiting there with their guns as the siege dragged on through the day. They had been told to take no part in the battle. They were confused, undirected. They now had no leader. When Constable Johnston was fetching straw and kerosene to set fire to the hotel, one of them raised a rifle. It is reputed to be Tom Lloyd who pushed the gun away and said: 'There has been enough killing.'[20]

But when the pub was burnt down and the two horribly charred bodies were raked from the ashes, these men moved in. There were so many of them that Superintendent Sadleir, although he now had fifty-one heavily armed policemen at Glenrowan, made no attempt to stop them. He realized that such a move would have been suicidal.

Now, added to the previous bitterness of these people, was the feeling of revenge. In July 1880, slightly less than a month after the capture of Ned Kelly and the destruction of the gang, Constable Baird at Eldorado saw Paddy Byrne, Joe Byrne's brother, riding eastward with Jim Kelly. The following day Paddy Byrne returned, riding toward the Woolshed with two brothers of Steve Hart. Baird commented, quite conservatively: 'It is evident that there is a stir among the sympathizers.'[21]

During those weeks and months, as the trial and execution of Ned Kelly approached, and his shot-mauled limbs gained strength, slowly the numbed, unco-ordinated body of sympathizers began to stir itself. Threats were made. Threats against Curnow, who stopped the police train; against the railway guard who had helped disarm the fallen Ned Kelly; against a splitter, William Williamson, one of the men convicted in the Fitzpatrick affair who later gave information against the Kellys. There were threats against Jack and Bill Sherritt who, to avenge their murdered brother, had galloped to Glenrowan with the police,

---

[20] Again, oral traditions of the sympathizers tally with police reports. Steele, in his report dated 10 August 1880 (Kelly Papers), quotes Johnston seeing a group of armed men. Sadleir also mentions the incident.

[21] Baird's report, dated 2 August 1880, is in the Kelly Papers.

carrying police shotguns. There were threats against Sergeant Steele, who applied to leave the district. (The request was refused!) Meanwhile, the situation at Greta was reaching crisis point.

Greta had, when all is said and done, been without police protection for two years. Senior Constable Kelly, one of the men who had played a prominent part in the capture of Ned Kelly, was posted to Greta, and refused to go. The plan was that he and three constables would be stationed at O'Brien's Hotel, which was the headquarters of the Kelly sympathizers. The police would be upstairs in their makeshift quarters while the sympathizers were drinking and swearing vengeance in the bar downstairs. Senior Constable Kelly had been married for three months and said that this was an utterly impossible posting. He described Greta as 'the most dangerous position in the district', and said that he would live in constant fear of ambush, inside the hotel and without.[22]

Sadleir was scathing: 'He pleaded to be excused from the fear of personal risk. . . . The Senior Constable's transfer was recommended as a mark of my disapproval of his conduct',[23] and he reported to Nicholson: 'I am obliged to employ an ordinary constable on a duty that this sub-officer does not think it prudent to undertake.'[24] The Constable he employed was Robert Graham, writer of the charming love letters which appear on pp. 86-88. Graham was a gentle, utterly dedicated police officer who had led an honest, unspectacular career. He was, however, distinguished by two characteristics: he was a very capable bushman and horseman, and he was a crack shot.

On 29 September, Robert Graham rode into Ned Kelly's home town, Greta, with three constables, all dressed in the bush clothes that troopers had worn throughout the Kelly outbreak. One can imagine them being watched from windows, from verandas, from behind trees, as they rode up to

[22] Royal Commission, Q.8290 *et seq.*
[23] Royal Commission, Q.8333.
[24] Royal Commission, Q.15950.

the pub with their pack horse. They went inside and took their swags upstairs. The men in the bar, silent, and watching, could hear the footsteps above. Then feet began to descend the stairs. Watched from the bar door, down the stairs came four men in the full uniform of the Victorian Mounted Police. Robert Graham was showing the people of Greta, in uncompromising terms, that the Law had returned to the Kelly country.[25]

As the day of Ned's execution approached, there was a massive distribution of police arms in the north-east. One hundred and sixty-two revolvers, eighty-nine shot guns, seventy-three rifles, twenty-seven carbines were distributed. The execution past, the members of the Kelly family returned to Greta, and uneasily, awkwardly, the brothers of the dead outlaws gathered there, almost like the ghosts of the Kelly gang, uncertain who had summoned them or why. Jim Kelly, talking to a trooper, said: 'I won't enter the bush. I've got a trade. I can earn three pounds a week by making boots.' Jim wanted an honourable peace. But he said: 'Should I ever be interfered with by the police, I will not do as Ned has done; I will shoot every man and have satisfaction.'[26]

Paddy Byrne was Joe's brother. But Joe was dead. There did not seem very much he could do. Shortly afterwards, he took up a gold claim on Reedy Creek with a couple of his mates. Dick Hart, Steve's brother, had stood beside the charred bodies at Glenrowan armed with a rifle, threatening to blow out the brains of the first man who tried to touch the bodies. No one could say that Dick had not done his duty by his brother, and there was work waiting on the Hart selection. Dick did not want any more trouble if it could be honourably avoided.

Slowly there began to be an easing off in the immediate

[25] The account of Graham's work at Greta is based on police records, Royal Commission Evidence (tragically, Graham was not called as a witness), on Graham's own scrapbook and letters, on the accounts of three of his surviving children, and on the family traditions of several sympathizers.

[26] Royal Commission, Q.12181.

pressure for revenge. But still there remained some uneasy ferment. Robert Graham began to probe the cause of this. It seemed incredible that though a gang of criminals had been destroyed, there was still a near-rebellion brewing in the district. Graham, who was a brilliant tactician and diplomat, bought a few bottles of brandy from the pub and started riding around the district, dropping in on old farmers and yarning with them. One of the farmers was Tom Lloyd Senior (not Tom Lloyd Junior's father, but his uncle) and it was this man, Ned Kelly's uncle, who, in a few simple words, told Graham what he desperately needed to know.

'The Kellys wanted ground,' he said. Now, the sympathizers wanted land, and, if they could be guaranteed access to that land, they would get rid of the few trouble-makers and hotheads remaining in the district.[27]

This was the vital breakthrough; the whole thing began to fall into place. Graham reported to Sadleir, who was delighted, and recommended Graham's promotion to Senior Constable. Sadleir was armed for an important interview. He writes:

One of the Kelly relatives, the prospective leader of the new gang, sought an interview with me when matters looked most threatening. My interviewer was pretty frank, not to say impudent, at first. When he was reminded of what happened to the Kelly gang and that, though a constable might be shot, the police went on for ever, he became more reasonable, and asked only that those of the Kelly circle who had taken up land should not be dispossessed. I was able to promise that no one who continued to obey the law would be interfered with, but that no further selections would be allowed to doubtful characters.[28]

[27] Accounts of this interview given by descendants of both men agree in detail.
[28] Sadleir *Recollections*.

With the root cause of the rebellion uncovered, it seemed only a matter of time before things could be placed on a stable basis in the Kelly country. But, in March 1881, came disaster. The Royal Commission into the Kelly outbreak began its sittings.

There were voluminous Press reports of the proceedings of the Royal Commission, including terrifying, ill-advised revelations about police informers and spies. From material published in newspapers, it was quite easy to identify people in the Kelly country who had been helping the police. Immediately the sympathizers burst forth into a wild witch-hunt, waiting for each day's newspapers, seeing if they could find another clue as to who had been helping to betray the gang. Things moved rapidly toward a crisis in Greta. The Acting Chief Commissioner of Police, H. M. Chomley, reported 'a very bad and revengeful feeling', and the threat of what he termed 'open acts of violence at any moment'.[29]

Inspector Montford was appointed Officer in Command of the north-east. Twelve constables were sent as reinforcements. Stanhope O'Connor was asked to re-organize the blacktrackers at Benalla. Robert Graham reported on April 24: 'A number of them were here yesterday drinking . . . and from their manner I am led to believe that another outbreak among them is imminent'.[30]

The previous day a dramatic telegram had arrived in Benalla:

Stolen last night from Acocks, Seven Mile Creek, two large pit saws supposed taken to construct armour of. Would be well to send trackers at once to Acocks, near Glenrowan. Will have tracks, if any, preserved.

(A. L. M. Steele.)[31]

Sergeant Steele, the man who had brought Ned Kelly

[29] Royal Commission, Appendix 4.
[30] Royal Commission, Q.9870.
[31] Royal Commission, Q.9870.

down at Glenrowan, now knew that the threat was real; the ghost of the Kelly gang had substance. Men who still had Kelly guns were now arming themselves with Kelly armour. That week the *Benalla Standard* reported:

> There is not the slightest doubt that the formation of another gang of bushrangers is being meditated in the Greta district. . . . Grave fears are being daily entertained of another outbreak.

Robert Graham was in a dangerous situation. He and his three troopers were living on a time bomb due to explode at any moment. Each night Graham slept with his revolver under his pillow. But he was a man of initiative, and, in his quiet way, he saw a possible solution.

At this point, we are again forced to rely on oral tradition. There was a priest who used to drink at O'Brien's Hotel (a man who is identified in police files). Graham approached him as a friend of the Kelly family and asked to be taken to meet Mrs Kelly and Jim. The priest agreed and we have, from several sources, descriptions of the sergeant and the priest (Graham was referred to as 'sergeant' around Greta) who kept calling at the Kelly homestead.

From this time, the rebellion subsided. There can be no doubt that on the personal representation of Robert Graham, Mrs Kelly and Jim moved among the sympathizers to dissuade them from this last act of madness, and prevent the ghastly, belated, futile finale to the Kelly outbreak.

During the first week in June, Inspector Montford visited Greta and talked to Robert Graham who, by a seeming miracle, had managed to contain the threatened outbreak. Montford already had plans to establish a new station on the Fifteen Mile Creek, about ten miles from Greta; and with four men there, four at Greta, and four at Glenrowan, a triangle of well-manned posts would surround the heart of the Kelly country. Graham explained his experience of moving among the people, gaining their trust. Montford, shortly after this, appeared before the Royal Commission and gave evidence behind closed doors, much of his material being based on the information given him by Graham a few days before. He mentioned these discussions and called Graham 'an exceedingly intelligent man, on whose judgement I can put great reliance'.

Montford outlined his recommendations for the North-Eastern district, the establishment of the new stations, the system of having well-known constables in constant movement among people of the district, and the administration of the Land Act through the police — a system which he described as 'a lever which would have more potency than an army of police'. Speaking of the Kelly sympathizers he told the Royal Commission: 'Their whole object is to obtain land'.[32]

Again, when peace was in sight, disaster once more threatened. Tom Lloyd Jnr. was refused a selection — according to family tradition, for the fifth time. Robert Graham interceded with a potent argument: 'How can you expect a man to lead an honest life when you deny him the only way he knows to earn a living?' Tom Lloyd was granted his selection.[33]

By the end of that year, 1881, the Kelly outbreak was at last over, and Robert Graham could bring his bride to Greta, to the town which only a few months before had been regarded as the 'worst place in the colony'. Graham, who in his letters had called the Kellys 'these villainous wretches', had since gained an enormous admiration for Ned Kelly, and a lifelong respect and affection for Mrs Kelly. He perhaps never knew the full story of the rebellion, but he sensed the important part of it.

The story of the Kelly rebellion, as we know it, is not conclusive. Many vital links are missing. But this paper represents an attempt — a first attempt, I believe — to bring some meaning to this mass of material, to reconcile documentary evidence with these frustrating fragments

[32] Royal Commission, Appendix 1.
[33] Again traditions of the Graham and Lloyd families coincide.

of verbal tradition which have come down to us. However, the basic facts emerge clearly. The Kellys were much more than mere criminals. Any attempt to interpret the escalation of the Kelly outbreak and the support afforded the Kelly gang as merely the results of a group of people supporting criminals in pursuit of criminal gain, is illogical. The gathering and turning back of the sympathizers at Glenrowan is irrefutable and, on this basis alone, we would be justified in saying that Ned Kelly, the man, was infinitely greater than his legend, a man of greater nobility and moral courage than anything we have even hinted at in the past.

*Question:* What do you make of the fact that there is evidence that Ned Kelly was not at his homestead at all during the day of the Fitzpatrick incident, but was somewhere in New South Wales?
*Jones:* I would like to be able to say that I have documentary evidence that Ned Kelly was 400 miles from Greta the day Fitzpatrick was shot. Unfortunately, I have documentary evidence that he was within riding distance of Greta that day. This is supplied by his own cousin.

At the trial of Mrs Kelly, Skillion and Williamson, Joe Ryan, Ned Kelly's cousin (subsequently one of the most prominent sympathizers) gave evidence that he had bought a horse from Ned Kelly for seventeen pounds on the day Fitzpatrick was shot. The dated receipt was produced in court. Coming from Ryan, I think we can regard this as conclusive proof of Kelly's whereabouts. What it *means* I do not know. I do not completely believe Fitzpatrick's story, and I can understand why Ned Kelly was prepared to lie about being in the district. He was clearly trying to discredit Fitzpatrick's story and protect his mother, his friend and his brother-in-law.

The whole business is terribly frustrating and one hates to admit defeat, but I cannot see any possibility of our ever knowing exactly what happened. But Kelly could have been there.

*Keith Dunstan:* Regarding the story of the rockets, Max Brown describes the sympathizers outside the hotel, but does not describe how they got there.

*Jones:* Brown, oddly enough, mentions both the rockets and the sympathizers galloping to Glenrowan, but does not develop or enlarge on these facts. I have gathered a strong body of oral tradition. Keith McMenomy was present at one of my interviews, with a gentleman who was prepared to talk about this. During other general interviews, I gained material from descendants of sympathizers, and from others. They substantiate the story in broad essentials, but differ on some details.

It must be remembered that this was a very confusing moment. All the men present, in fact, were guilty of treason. It is easy to see why this is the most closely guarded secret of the Kelly story.

If you want documentary evidence of the rockets, I refer you to Question 11,190 of the Minutes of Evidence of the Royal Commission, the evidence of Constable Arthur, who described seeing the rockets and was questioned briefly about them. He replied: 'If you want to know about the rockets, ask Constable Gascoigne'. Unfortunately, no one did!

Curnow himself heard 'the galloping of many hooves' coming from the Greta stronghold. Sadleir, Johnston, Steele and many other police described the sympathizers in the bush behind the police lines. Sadleir himself identifies these men as 'armed friends of the outlaws who were preparing to join them for a raid on a bank'. We may choose to regard this as all they planned to do. I do not really think so. Everything indicates that it was something much bigger; inseparable from the concept of something approaching a Republic of Victoria, a major revolution, not merely a criminal act.

*Question:* This is not so much a question as a statement, but I think it supports your analysis of the situation regarding the discontent of the selectors. If we go back some years prior to Glenrowan, to the time of the Lands Convention regarded as prior to representative government (a form of Shadow Government), I think it was one of the leaders, Wilson Graveden (?), who said: 'For every man a vote, a farm, and a rifle to protect his farm.'

*Jones:* We should not underestimate the feelings that were stirred up among the selectors by the existence of what was called in the Royal Commission the 'Black List'. No man whose name was on the Black List could own ground in Kelly country. It is also significant that one of the papers (*The Sketcher,* I believe), reporting the arrest of the sympathizers, said: 'Most appeared to be of the labouring class but describe themselves as farmers and selectors.' Many of them were exactly this, potential farmers who had not yet taken out selections of their own.

It was a pattern for young men to travel around the country shearing and doing general bush work, before settling down on their own selections. They would stay on the family property until after they left school, then go shearing, timber cutting, droving, until they decided to set up home. Men like these would be hardest hit by this 'Black List'. And these were potentially the most valued members of the Kelly gang, young fellows in their late teens and early twenties, hot-headed, ready to fight. And now, they had been given something to fight about.

*Keith Dunstan:* Recently, when M. H. Ellis, writing in *The Bulletin,* accused Kelly of being a coward, the basis of his accusation was that Kelly deserted his mates. Could you tell me exactly when Kelly saw these rockets, as this seems the crux of the situation?

*Jones:* It happened, we know exactly, from Constable Arthur's evidence, at the time of the second volley from the police. Superintendent Hare and the police had left the train. Bracken had met them and told them the Kellys were in the pub. Bracken had immediately ridden off to Wangaratta for help.

The police ran up the slope toward the inn and, as they approached it, the gang opened fire from the veranda. The first volley hit Hare. The police returned the fire and wounded Kelly. Presumably, the Kellys fired again almost immediately, and the police returned their fire.

It was after this second volley that the sympathizer with the rockets moved. The rockets were fired between the railway station and McDonald's Tavern, just about the middle of the Hume Highway as it exists today. That is the exact time and place. Ned Kelly was outside the hotel at this stage. He had previously mounted Music, the grey mare, to ride down to the line, and on his return he dismounted and turned Music into the horse paddock. Seeing the rockets, he apparently mounted her again with some difficulty and left — presumably by the back gate of the horse paddock — to head down around the lower slopes of Morgan's Lookout towards the gap leading towards Wangaratta. He was already quite seriously wounded but, immediately on seeing the rockets, went to head off the sympathizers.

*Question:* Did he ride his mare wearing his armour?

*Jones:* Yes, incredible as it may seem. It is a small detail, but apparently, it was not *his* mare; Music, the grey, was Joe Byrne's mare. Ned's mare was a chestnut called Mirth which carried the Kelly brand of the 'E and reversed K conjoined'. After the Jerilderie robbery, Ned Kelly appeared riding Joe Byrne's grey mare Music, and this was the horse he continued to ride until captured. Not only did he ride Music during the night of the siege, but Music followed him throughout the last stand. Music was seen trotting through the bush behind him and, as I quoted last night from Sergeant Steele, actually passed between Ned Kelly and Steele in the closing moments of the fight.

*Weston Bate:* As custodian of the historical context of this exercise, I would like to question whether the 1870s as you depicted them were quite what they really were; in particular with regard to the Berry Administration. It need not have been short of money; and this was not a time of depression. There was a battle between the Upper House and the Lower House over payment of members. Berry was virtually refusing supply unless the Upper House let his bill go through. This is the reason for Black Wednesday when the problem of the Public Service arose. When the Upper House vetoed the bill Berry decided to economize by sacking most of the senior public servants.

*Jones:* In going through the Press reports from 1875 to 1880, you will find a constant reiteration of depression, falling gold yield, bad seasons. The *Ovens and Murray Advertiser* from 1875 onwards gives a detailed picture of the situation in the district — graft, embezzlement, bankruptcy, and so on.

*Weston Bate:* You get bankruptcy in some of the best times too, and you get local areas with this sort of problem. But, as far as the State as a whole is concerned, I do not think you can talk about a general problem of insolvency.

Moreover, in many ways this is the best time for selectors in Victoria. The majority of them were on their feet, and were able to withstand many of the problems which would have hit them very hard some years earlier like the bad seasons you mention. This does not, of course, invalidate your thesis about people around Greta, or any group who were suddenly caught by the Kelly situation and were moved to rebellion, because they were, on the whole, people who were being left out. It is possible to see a minority in the situation, but not a general depression.

*Jones:* I am surprised to hear this. I have a dozen or more references showing a continuous development of this theme. You find it stated very well in *The Sketcher* where the whole thing is condensed into a weekly report. To me, the picture is quite clear. We are in happy disagreement.[1]

*Question:* Has the story that Ned Kelly had the idea of kidnapping the Governor any basis at all?

*Jones:* This is a strong tradition, and has been linked with

[1] [*Weston Bate:*] The area of disagreement may not be as great as at first appeared. I have no objection to an interpretation of the late 70s which emphasizes a general *recession* (but not a 'depression') in the Victorian economy, coupled with particularly severe local stress in the Kelly country. The reason for the Berry government's sacking of public servants is not as important as the fact that they were sacked, and I think that Ian Jones's hypothesis that Constable Fitzpatrick felt compelled to show evidence of zeal to his superiors is a logical result of the situation.

the Glenrowan campaign. There are stories that there were sympathizers in Melbourne watching the movements of the Marquis of Normanby. Bishop Moorhouse was also spoken of as a potential hostage.

*Question:* What strength can we give to the story that Ned Kelly, at Jerilderie, saw a schoolchild in the street and said: 'Here's a shilling young man. Go and tell your school-mates there'll be no school today. The schoolteacher won't be coming. What's your name?'

'Jackie,' the child replied.

'Jackie who?'

'Jackie Monash.'

*Jones:* Another one of 'the marvellous traditions. Unfortunately, Monash was going to Scotch College at this stage, and apparently had gone back to school before the Jerilderie hold-up. But, I'd rather believe the story, I must admit.[2]

*M. Moonie [Albury Border Mail]:* Would you care to state the number of the force of sympathizers that would have arisen if Kelly had not turned them back at Glenrowan?

*Jones:* I have no idea. I imagine the movement could have gained considerable support. The concept of a guerrilla force operating in the north-east is a terrifying one. These men were far better bushmen than the police who could be brought against them. This was a constant source of worry during the whole police pursuit. Many of the men posted to the district were not countrymen; they were from the metropolis and provincial cities. It was said: 'The men who knew the country died at Stringybark Creek.' There were two crack bushmen in the pursuit — Johnston and Lawless. Apart from these two men, the gang had the edge on the police.

Looking at the possible Kelly rebellion, there are parallels with Eureka. There is the factor of the Russian scare at the time of Eureka, and the one at the time of the Kelly

---

[2] *[Ian Jones:]* I have since learned that Monash himself confirmed the story—and spoke highly of the advice given him by Ned Kelly in a brief chat.

outbreak — each playing its own role in shaping the destinies of the rebels. But, at Eureka there were half-asleep, half-armed rebels against crack redcoats. The Kelly outbreak was the reverse. There would have been a crack guerrilla force, well-armed, fighting on their own terms, against a force of police armed, in the words of the Royal Commission, 'like a Turkish Brigade'. I do not know where it would have led. Against them could only have been put the garrison artillery and the militia.

*Question:* I have read that there was a girl who helped Ned Kelly, Jenny Macdonald. Is this story true?

*Jones:* There was some love interest in the Kelly story. Kelly was, as far as I can find, engaged at the time of his execution. There is a verbal tradition that he was secretly married. That I cannot yet prove, but the existence of the girl — and her identity — are indisputable. The name Jenny Macdonald is fictitious. In fact, none of the candidates yet put forward qualifies — certainly not poor little Jane Jones. She was a sickly fifteen-year-old who possibly worshipped Ned, but I do not think her fervour was reciprocated. It has been claimed recently that 'a police bullet killed Ned Kelly's girl'. While Jane Jones did suffer a very slight wound at the siege, she died of natural causes two years later. I have her death certificate.

*Question:* Sadleir's book describes Constable McIntyre as 'a God-fearing, devout man'. Do you think this type of man would stand up in a court of law, commit perjury and swear a man's life away?

*Jones:* I could not say what any man — God-fearing or otherwise — would do under these circumstances. McIntyre had been through hell, and I am not at all convinced that the disparities in McIntyre's stories were his own idea. I hesitate to suggest that McIntyre could have been influenced by superiors, but this is possible. I don't think McIntyre was a coward as has been claimed. I believe he did the only possible thing under the circumstances, exactly as Ned Kelly said.

It is impossible to escape the fact that Constable Mc-

Intyre gave to Superintendent Sadleir an account of the shooting of Lonigan which exactly matched Ned Kelly's account, before Ned Kelly's account had been uttered or published. He described Lonigan running to a log, dropping behind it, coming up to fire, and then being shot. It is also impossible to escape the fact that this does not tally with any other account McIntyre gave of the shooting, including that given at the Kelly trial. Perjury is a very hard word. But, a man's life was at stake; and I think that even if a man's honour is involved, the life is more important than the honour.

# 7

# Kelly — The Criminal

## KEITH HOLDEN

*Sergeant Keith Holden was Public Relations Officer for the Victoria Police until 1970 and is currently Grounds Co-Ordinator, Melbourne University. He has made an extensive study of the police records of the pursuit and capture of Ned Kelly.*

A great deal has already been said about Ned Kelly as a man, and the evidence is conclusive that he did in fact have many remarkable qualities. That he had a commanding presence, a tough physique, a handsome appearance, an ability to capture an audience, and a certain charm with the ladies, cannot be denied. Nor can it be denied that he was clever and capable of executing well organized raids against the community. But if we look at his record and examine his activities purely in the light of his inability to live within the law, we find that he also has most of the attributes of a cunning, scheming, vicious criminal equal to the worst of his kind today.

While we must sympathize with the individual whose domestic environment and circumstances were such that poverty and hardship were their everyday problems, we cannot condone behaviour which is against the accepted standards of the community, nor can we make a hero of one who would kill and rob to achieve his ends.

It is also human nature to feel sympathy for one who is outlawed by society and on the run for his life from the enforcers of the law. Perhaps one could admire Kelly's skill in making his pursuers appear foolish by so easily eluding them, but it must be accepted that one man cannot hold a whole State to ransom without paying the penalties of the law. Kelly was costing a young developing country thousands of pounds which it could ill afford, and tied up the activities of hundreds of police for almost two years.

Perhaps we should review his unlawful activities to see just how often he was the subject of the processes of law.

| | | |
|---|---|---|
| 14 October 1869 | Charged with assault and robbery with violence | Dismissed |
| 5 May 1870 | Charged with Highway robbery (two counts) as an accomplice of Harry Power, bushranger | Dismissed |
| 30 October 1870 | Charged with Assault | Convicted. 3 months' imprisonment |
| 30 October 1870 | Charged with Indecent behaviour | Convicted. 3 months' imprisonment |
| 16 April 1871 | Charged with Receiving a horse | Convicted. 3 years' imprisonment |
| 14 September 1877 | Charged with Drunkenness riding on the footpath resisting arrest | Convicted and fined £3/1/- |
| 15 March 1878 | Warrants issued by Sgt. Steele for arrest of Ned Kelly for horse-stealing | |
| 26 October 1878 | Murders of Constables Lonigan, Scanlon and Sergeant Kennedy | |
| 1 November 1878 | Kelly gang outlawed. £4,000 reward offered | |
| 10 December 1878 | Armed holdup and robbery of Euroa National Bank | |
| 8 February 1879 | Armed holdup and robbery of Jerilderie Bank of N.S.W. | |
| 9 February 1879 | Reward increased to £8,000 | |
| 27 June 1880 | Murder of Aaron Sherritt by Joe Byrne (member of the Kelly gang) | |
| 29 June 1880 | Kelly captured at Glenrowan | |
| 28 October 1880 | Kelly charged with murder of Constable Lonigan | |
| 29 October 1880 | Kelly found guilty and sentenced to death | |
| 11 November 1880 | Kelly hanged in Old Melbourne Jail | |

191

In addition to the listed offences above, Kelly openly stated to the assembled gathering at Younghusbands station, outside Euroa, that he had stolen some 280 head of horses and cattle over the previous few years and had taken them to New South Wales to sell them. With these offences he was never charged. This then, is the record of a man who is idolized by many as one who dared to oppose the oppressors and show his disdain of authority.

Yet if we look further at some of the incidents in his short life we shall see that many of them have no reason to be glorified and that they were indeed petty and mundane.

In the affair of Ah Fook, whom he robbed and assaulted, police evidence was given that the Chinese did indeed have bruising and abrasions on his body. It is likely that it was only the evidence concocted and supported by three of Kelly's friends and relations, against the unsupported story of the Chinese, which enabled Kelly to get the case dismissed. One can hardly imagine a small Chinese endeavouring to make trouble in the stronghold of the notorious Kelly family.

Kelly, by his own admission, was with Harry Power on numerous occasions when this old villain held up travellers, but he was only charged with two of these offences and was lucky to have them dismissed against him.

We see a different side of Kelly when we consider the incident with McCormack, the hawker, and his wife, when an argument arose regarding the using of McCormack's horse. Kelly, who at this time was a strapping youth, openly admitted having savagely attacked the hawker. For this he received three months' imprisonment, and in the same court on the same day he was further charged and sentenced to a further three months' imprisonment for indecent behaviour. This charge resulted from Kelly's having had a lad deliver a parcel containing a pair of calves' testicles to the childless Mrs McCormack, with a note suggesting that the contents of the parcel might be of some use to her.

If he did ever grow into the state of being a gentleman, as has been suggested, it certainly did not stem from these beginnings. Nor do we see great evidence of refinement when he was carried off to Benalla lock-up and charged with the most common of offences — drunk in a public place.

After being released from Pentridge, Kelly worked as a timber cutter for about two years, then, finding that he could not settle down, tried his hand at prospecting. He soon found that it was a more profitable business to steal the horses and cattle with which the countryside abounded at that time. And so, the inevitable occurred: Kelly was named as a horse-thief and a warrant was taken out against him. This was never executed as the next time the police got their hands on him, it was for the murder for which he was hanged.

In the month after the horse-stealing warrant was taken out, a fracas developed when Constable Fitzpatrick was endeavouring to arrest Kelly. The result was that warrants were issued against Mrs Kelly, her sons, Ned and Dan, William Williamson, and William Skillion for attempted murder of the constable in the execution of his duty.

From that moment, the Kelly gang was constantly on the run from the police and the pinnacle of their criminal career was reached with the ambushing and shooting of the three police at Stringybark Creek. Perhaps understandable was the shooting of Constable Lonigan, who immediately drew his revolver and fired at Kelly. Perhaps one could also understand the shooting of Constable Scanlon who, when bailed up, made a hasty attempt to unsling his Spencer rifle with the obvious intention of shooting Kelly; but when we review Kelly's actions in relation to Sergeant Kennedy we get a better idea of his low criminal mind. When Kennedy was wounded, minus his revolver and on the run, Kelly and his brother Dan pursued him through the bush like a hunted animal, finally shooting him through the heart as he lay bleeding on the ground and unable to move. Kelly, in recounting the story later, claimed that he

193

shot him because he did not want Sergeant Kennedy to suffer. If ever there was an act of cold-blooded murder, it was this one. Not content with this, the gang then robbed the body of the Sergeant's gold watch. And although Kelly did not and probably would not admit to so low a deed, the autopsy revealed that the Sergeant's ears had been cut from his head. In denying these charges in his Jerilderie letter, Kelly probably realized that he had performed an act which further outraged the public.

The following is an extract of the Mansfield Occurrence book:

9th November, Saturday, at 4 p.m. Mrs Monks reported receiving a threatening letter of which the following is a copy:

To E. Monks, You think you have done a great thing by searching for the traps but you have made a great mistake, for your friend Kennedy is gone although we made him confess many things and many little things you have told him in confidence and we heard you say you could trust us and our horns, but we will trust you to hell but what we will have you. We will make your place a Government camp when we come and give you some more bodies to pack. What a fine thing it is to cut their ears off, but we will poke your eyes out. Yours until we meet

Edward and Daniel Kelly

With his skilfully executed raids on the banks at Euroa and Jerilderie, Kelly showed a great deal of native cunning and also a certain degree of leadership. However, his Jerilderie raid appears to have been launched purely in order to have the disjointed ravings of his Jerilderie Letter published for all to see.

The now famous Kelly armour — manufactured of mouldboards stolen from ploughs — is adequate proof of Kelly's determination to flout the law and challenge its upholders. It is a grim reminder that he did not intend to be taken alive and that he would retaliate against those who would bring him to justice for his crimes. Evidence also of the extent to which he was prepared to break the law was the tearing up of the railway lines at Glenrowan in order to wreck the police special train, and his stated intention of shooting any of the police who survived when the train plunged into the gully.

Again, the taking of life and destruction of property meant little to him.

When it came to the final show-down and the battle at Glenrowan, we find an anti-climax to the whole affair when we discover that the leader was not even at the scene for most of the time, when his gang needed him as never before. While his brother Dan and Steve Hart were lying dead in the hotel and his friend Joe Byrne was bleeding to death, Kelly was skulking in the bush somewhere behind the hotel, and there is some evidence that he was in a drunken stupor. The expression, 'as game as Ned Kelly' arose because he returned to the fight, but he really had very little choice. Unable to get out of his heavy armour or mount his horse, his only hope of obtaining assistance was to join his mates in the hotel. Taking advantage of the early morning mists, he came towards the hotel from behind the police lines, only to be quickly captured by Sergeant Steele.

A saga of lawlessness such as the State had never seen before or since was over. But the stories and writings have continued until Kelly has achieved almost hero-like proportions. Perhaps this has occurred because no official point of view has ever been presented to show the extent of his criminal activities.

That Sir Redmond Barry considered justice to have been done can be in little doubt as this letter to the Governor after the trial confirms:

His Excellency the Governor of Victoria.
Sir,
I have the honour to report for the information of

your Excellency and the Executive Council that the Prisoner was tried before me on Thursday and Friday in this week for the Wilful murder of Thomas Lonigan a constable at the Wombat ranges creek on Saturday, the 26th of October.

He was found Guilty and sentenced to death.

The History of the prisoner during the last two years and the numerous criminal acts with which he admitted on several occasions to different people he was connected are sufficiently well known to render it unnecessary for me to say more than that the case was amply proved and that I see no reason whatever to recommend that the sentence should not be carried into execution.

My notes of the evidence will be forwarded without delay.

I have the honour to be,
　　Your Excellency's most obedient servant,
　　　*Sgd* Redmond Barry
　　Senior puisne judge of the Colony of Victoria
　　　Supreme Court Oct 30th 1880.

Police work has changed little since Kelly's time and the police still pay particular attention to trouble-makers who have previously come to their notice, and especially to the ringleader. Once he is removed from the scene the 'fight' normally goes out of the others very quickly.

Police must act where there are grounds for suspicion, and, in Kelly's case and on his own admissions of horse and cattle duffing and highway robbery, there were very strong grounds indeed.

Superintendent Nicholson's instruction to the police echoed the policy of police enforcement principles of today. He said, 'I expressed my opinion to the officer in charge of the district that, without oppressing the people, or worrying them in any way, he should endeavour whenever they commit any paltry crime, to bring them to justice, and send them to Pentridge even on a paltry sentence, the object being to take their prestige away from them.

'This has as good effect as being sent to prison with very heavy sentences because the prestige those men get up there, from what is termed 'flashness' helps to keep them together, and that is a very good way of taking the flashness out of them.'

The laws of 1870 were little different from those of today, but Kelly sought to contest them through those whose duty it was to uphold them, rather than to try to right the wrongs which he believed existed.

Then, as now, unpopular laws had to be enforced, and it was the police who bore the brunt of individual and community antagonism.

In 1829, Sir Richard Mayne stated:

The primary object of an efficient police is the prevention of crime; the next that of detection and punishment of offenders, if crime is committed.

To these ends all efforts of the police must be directed. The protection of life and property, the preservation of public tranquillity and the absence of crime will alone prove whether these efforts have been successful, and whether the objects for which the police were appointed have been attained.

Little is heard of the families of the policemen who were shot by Kelly at Stringybark, and although there were public subscriptions and expressions of sympathy at the time, we hear far more sympathy expressed for Kelly and his gang. Who were the real victims of the battle? Those whose duty it was to preserve law and order or those who defied the law of the land and had been outlawed for their efforts?

Mr Justice Dunphy, referring in recent years to a book on Kelly, wrote:

I am afraid that I cannot agree with any conclusion which attempts to make Kelly out anything else but a natural and confirmed criminal. It is quite a conventional approach to attempt to excuse or even vindicate criminals by dealing with their early environment and blaming their lapses upon outside social influences.

In some instances there is some justification for a plea of this type but there is rarely any substance in an argument advanced on behalf of any individual guilty of habitual violence. The best that can be said for criminals of this type is that they were born that way, but such a plea is of little satisfaction to society generally and to the relatives of murdered men in particular.

I was Crown Solicitor in Western Australia for seven years and during that time was concerned with all the major trials, these included cases of murder, rape and aggravated assault, and almost without exception the accused person at some time or other attempted to justify himself in the same way as did the Kellys. There is extraordinary similarity between the verbiage of the hard-luck stories of modern criminals I have known and Kelly's own attempted excuses for his conduct.

The best thing I could say about bushrangers was that they undoubtedly had ample courage and they certainly took risks which in a better sphere would have entitled them to a major decoration. At the same time some of their crimes were callous and cowardly murders. This contrast is a characteristic of the predestined habitual criminal, who seems to have an inexplicable mixture of reckless bravery and callous and cowardly brutality.

In a Democracy where the laws are made by the people for the people and generally for the health and safety of the people, the role of the police is to see that the law is kept; it is useless for the public to attack the police because it does not approve of the current laws. The police are duty bound to enforce existing laws until they are changed by the Legislature. And because of our legal system, there is a heavy responsibility on the community to assist, indeed at common law they commit offences if they do not.

Kelly, by the viciousness and extent of his activities,

caused the Legislature to enact a special Act of Parliament proclaiming him an outlaw so that the whole community would rally to bring him to heel. This action, unprecedented in Victoria, was necessary to help the police to restore peace and tranquillity in the State.

I find that modern young people have very little knowledge of the true Kelly story, only knowing vaguely of Kelly as a bushranger who wore fantastic armour. I hope that the police viewpoint on Kelly will help to show that he was, if nothing else, a criminal.

# Appendix: Letters

Sir,

My Uncle George Kennedy was a great friend of Det. Roche who followed Butler to America. Here is the start and finish from him:

1. Mrs Kelly was running Kate Kelly for all she could to marry the Policeman.

2. The morning of the tragedy Mrs Kelly sent for the policeman and he came, she told him he had Kate in family way and what was he going to do about it. He denied he was responsible Dan Kelly was shoeing a horse as he and Ned were going away prospecting for about 6 weeks. Ned Kelly was out on the common looking for the 2 pack horses. Mrs Kelly said to Dan he has Kate in trouble and said he won't marry her. Dan said to him you are not much of a man if you won't. He challenged Dan to fight and Dan took him on. He beat Dan. Ned Kelly came trotting into the yard with the 2 pack horses. Mrs Kelly told him what was the cause of the trouble. The Policeman said get off your horse and I will clean you up too and Ned got off and bashed the Policeman. Policeman said I am going to see the Sergeant. Ned made up his mind that if they came back to arrest him after challenging him to fight, he would shoot the two of them. Ned went into the front room to watch and clean the revolver. Back they came — if policemen were going to arrest in those days they would kick the gate open. They kicked it open and Ned shot the two of them. Ned and Dan cleared away on horse back all day. They decided to use that high hill between Glenrowan and the border left-hand side of train line going to Melbourne.

They could see for miles around. They came back at night and picked up their supplies they were going to use prospecting. If you were to go up that mountain now you might find some bit of cave they used in wet weather, or where the horses were tied up. Mick Savage was working after school hours until 11 o'clock at night in the Glenrowan store when he became Prime Minister of New Zealand in 1935. Kate must have wrote to him to compliment him. He took her to N.Z. bought nice place on the outskirts of Auckland. In 1939 the place was pointed out to me and I was told she then would be 83 years of age.

P. Bryant
12.2.67

P.S. In those days both sides would keep it quiet — a girl was in the family way. So it was put down to horse duffing as the charge. You won't unravel anything with modern methods. If you don't understand the protection given to a girl in those days by both sides.

Dear Sir,

As a child 12 years of age during the end of First World War, I knew a woman well, who was later accused or questioned in the Goondwindi Police Court, as being Kate Kelly. The matter arose over some simple offence when this woman was giving evidence in Court. At the time she assured the Court, that she was only 10 years of age when the Kelly gang was operating.

This woman was known to me as Mrs Wallace, being then between 50 and 55 years of age. She also claimed her first husband was Ambrose and that her maiden name was Livingstone. I believe she would have been at least 10 years of age when the Kelly gang came into existence, and I think she was born near Corowa N.S.W. She had told me on more than one occasion she had left bags containing groceries etc. at appointed places where Ned Kelly or his gang could obtain the food without detection, during their bushranging days. She also told me the full history as to why Ned became a bushranger, from their side of course.

Furthermore this woman would be the greatest horse-woman in her younger days Australia has ever seen or known. I personally assisted her when she opened up several trunks of prizes, such as ribbons, cards, trophies, cups etc. which she had won at the various shows and race tracks — mainly in N.S.W. and Victoria — Ned Kelly country. She obtained permission for a tent site in the Goondwindi show grounds and charged 2/- per head for the public to view these prizes. I assisted in collecting these 2/- pieces whilst she explained to the Public, as to how she won these various prizes which filled a good size tent.

At this time Mrs Wallace had a property about 40 miles north of Goondwindi called Black Springs and she was assisted on this property by a Steve Peblwich (surname may not be spelt correctly). I can recollect her telling her story on several occasions and how she told me her secret that she knew Dan Kelly was still living then and that he had actually escaped the shanty fire near Glenrowan or Wangaratta where the Kelly gang made their last stand in June 1880. She told how an unknown person had become drunk before the alarm and that it was this man's remains the police later took to be Dan Kelly's. Dan had actually been burnt somewhat in the fire and had made his escape. Some few miles away a German farmer with whom he was acquainted looked after him until all died down and he later left the locality, letting the Authorities believe he was killed in the fire.

I have recollections of Mrs Wallace saying that Dan would one day claim his correct identity.

Dan Kelly was alleged at that time to be working on station property in either the Goondwindi or Warwich districts under an assumed name.

Many years passed, I believe about the end of the 2nd World War, a man came to light — I think he was in the B.G. Hospital at the time when he claimed to be Dan Kelly the outlaw. There was some investigations mainly by Reporters of Papers.

It was a foregone conclusion of the outcome. The

Authorities claimed it was untrue that Dan Kelly's remains had been accounted for in the shanty fire.

Later it came out that this old fellow, a tramp who was train-jumping near Ipswich had stood up an open wagon and struck an overhead bridge — so in my opinion this was the true end of Dan Kelly, brother of Ned.

I am not supplying my name but this, as far as my recollections go is true in every detail — this probably would at the time of Dan Kelly's death, supported his statement that he was Dan Kelly. I cannot remember having heard at any time under what name Dan Kelly went under after his escape.

[Unsigned]
12/3/67.

Sir,

Now approaching 80 years of age I grew in the 'Kelly Area.' My Grandfather was on staff at Beechworth gaol, living in quarters with his family i.e. wife, son and 3 daughters. A prisoner would be detailed to help in the kitchen — so the children came to know well the appearance etc. of some of the prisoners. One in particular I heard of, Steve Hart aged 16 in for sheep stealing.

During Ned Kelly's trial at Beechworth, grandfather carried Kelly from cell to cab to be taken to court, reversing procedure at end of days sittings. I do not remember if Dan Kelly or Joe Byrne were prisoners in gaol before the Kelly trial — or for that matter Ned Kelly.

As my Grandfather told it Joe Byrne was the most troublesome as far as control of the gang by Ned Kelly was concerned — not a great respecter of women etc.

Constable Fitzpatrick was sent to Kellys home to arrest Ned and Dan — was told by Mrs Kelly they were not home but Fitzpatrick would search the place. In an outbuilding Mrs Kelly found Fitzpatrick fooling around her daughter Kate so to show her displeasure struck the Constable on the helmet with I think a stable broom putting a big dent in

203

the helmet. Fitzpatrick rode away towards the barracks — later shot himself in left wrist, fell off, or got off the horse, which returned to barracks — this being noticed a detail was sent to backtrack towards the Kelly's home. They met with Fitzpatrick whose tale was 'finding the Kellys were not at home he started to return to barracks and later meeting Dan and Ned Kelly endeavoured to effect their arrest. As they resisted he drew his revolver but was shot in left arm. Fell off horse, which then ran away'. On the statement the Kellys were outlawed.

It was known Ned, Dan and Joe Byrne were part of the gang; they were not sure of the fourth until a posse followed a trail which it lost towards Bright. It was realized only one man knew the district well enough to lose the posse — Steve Hart.

The night Aaron Sherritt was shot my Mother and aunt were returning to quarters accompanied by either young warders or police when 4 horsemen were heard coming along the road between the jail and police station. My aunt said rather loudly 'that's the Kelly gang'. The horses were reined almost to a stop, then eased into a canter and away. This road was used to go towards Chiltern-Albury.

Aaron Sherritt was shot by Joe Byrne as was also Sgt. Kennedy. Shooting Sherritt they used a German who lived near to Sherritt to call Aaron to be shown the track to his hut, he was supposed to be or was drunk. Sherritt opened the door, was shot by Byrne. The two police at the hut — one dived under the bed, the other into the chimney. Sherritts wife (not long married) maiden name was I think Johanna Maher. To catch the Kelly gang police camps were set out in the bush. The one where Byrne shot Sgt. Kennedy was found by the Kellys by discarded food tins reflecting the sunlight.

As the Kellys rode towards this cave-camp, they intercepted the two relief policemen, Scanlon and Londrigan (distant relatives I think) going towards camp, where those in camp were not alert thinking the approaching horses and men would be the relief. I think the camp was bailed up. Kennedy tried to arrest the 2 Kellys and Byrne shot the Sergeant.

At Glenrowan Hotel the Kelly gang took charge as they wanted no warning to be given to the train from Melbourne with troopers and black trackers, rails had been removed nearer Melbourne.

During the evening the local schoolteacher (Curnow) came to the hotel was allowed in then told Ned Kelly he had come for spirits for his wife who was ill. On his promising he would not mention that the Kellys were holding prisoner all in the hotel he was allowed to go despite protests by Joe Byrne. On reaching home the teacher took a lamp and his wife's red shawl and walked along the rail line towards Melbourne, finally stopped the pilot engine and train from an accident. The police and trackers surrounded the hotel and opened fire on the occupants. On the train as a passenger was a priest, Rev. Fr. Gibney. He was later allowed to approach the hotel carrying a white flag. His purpose to help those possibly dying. While all interest was on Fr. Gibney, the police crept to rear of hotel setting it on fire.

Ned Kelly got away from the hotel and missing Joe Byrne returned to hotel to look for him and found him dead. Again trying to escape he was shot in the leg or legs and captured. He knew Dan and Steve Hart had escaped so far. Byrne's body was tied to a post at Glenrowan police station and photographed. Ned Kelly was brought to Beechworth jail. Whilst there was tried and transferred to Melbourne for future trial and hanging. This was necessary to allow the police to regain face after being the laughing stock of the area, particularly when the police at station was bailed up, then put in cells and the Kelly gang in police uniforms held up a bank and took prisoners with them to Younghusbands station. The joke 'Why are the Kelly gang good matchmakers?' 'They took young women to young husbands'. Kelly's sentence to death was a foregone conclusion. Mrs Kelly, Mother of Ned and Dan was in jail without trial.

My uncle a mining engineer was in South Africa during the Boer War. He met Dan Kelly and Steve Hart — they were fighting with the Boers — they remembered him.

The Mother of Aaron Sherritt used to cart dray loads of firewood into Beechworth using 2 horses, 1 in shafts, 1 as leader. This one was a dirty grey — called Dick and could open any garden gate when hungry. Brothers Hugh and Nesbit cut and delivered firewood (logs) to Zwar's Tannery.

I can remember a man charged with sheep stealing. His legs had been amputated. He sat in a wheel chair — cutting the ear marks off sheeps ears when arrested, about 30 sheep. I think Kelly was hung in Melbourne jail, a place where Deemings ghost was often reported as being seen and described by warders who had never heard of him. No Kelly ghost. This is about all my memory re the Kelly gang.

[Unsigned]
March, 1967.


Sir,
As a Kelly sympathizer I feel that although much has been said and written about Ned Kelly, few efforts have been made to get behind, or rather inside, the man to inquire into the real nature of his challenge to authority. It was no blind, irrational and purposeless interlude in the history of this land. I do not agree with Kelly's detractors that he was an illiterate inarticulate lout. His campaign against the squatters' state of Victoria had the touch of military genius; as any good soldier he was ruthless towards his enemies, but it was the nature of his rebellion that made the men of property, through their government, take the ultimate measures to put down the Kellys, even before the clash at Stringybark Creek. The retort of Judge Barry to Mrs Kelly at her trial leaves no room for doubt on this point: 'If your son Ned were here I would make an example of him for the whole of Australia — I would give him 15 years.'

Ned Kelly was intelligent and politically aware. He saw in the colonial set-up in the Colony of Victoria a parallel with the landed system at home in Ireland, where a dispossessed peasantry warred with their landlords or their landlords' agents. Perhaps Kelly identified himself as the champion of the Irish tenant farmer's Australian counterpart — the small selector?

Another important factor was the police force at the time. The Irish contempt for the police stems from the fact that in Ireland the alien government maintained its order not merely by an army of occupation, but by a large paramilitary police force, the Royal Irish Constabulary, which was recruited from native born Irishmen. A policeman then to an Irish nationalist was no more than a collaborator with 'the enemy,' one who was always prepared to do England's 'dirty work.' This attitude might be summed up by the remark of an Irish friend, a man of no mean birth or education, when he remarked of another Irishman, 'He's no bloody good anyway; his father was a policeman.'

This attitude towards the police found justification in Australia, where colonial governments maintained police troopers with a large Irish membership. The principal actors in the Kelly drama were Irishmen. Even the judge, Redmond Barry, was Irish, of the very class that transported John Kelly, the father of Ned and Dan, for a crime against their state; and this judge had passed judgement on the Kellys before they were outlawed for their crimes against the colonial State of Victoria.

There is an Irish song of defiance, which expresses the Kelly outlook—'The Felons of our Land,' (copy attached). In occupied Ireland felony was mainly committed against the alien government and what it stood for. An Irish felon was the same as an Irish patriot: 'The felon's cap's the noblest crown an Irish head can wear,' explains Ned Kelly better than my poor efforts. I don't mean that Ned regarded himself as a transported Irishman; he was an Australian and saw himself as such, but carrying on the fight against the old enemy, the men of wealth and property, in the new

land. It was this identification with the poor selectors, or
their identification with him, in their struggle for land on
which to build a new nation, that created popular sympathy
for the Kellys. Ned Kelly was the wish-fulfilment of the
battlers, doing the deeds they would like to have done had
they the courage and ability, he represented them and their
cause. This is the stuff from which folk heroes and legends
are made.

[E. Sheeham]
18/8/67.

The symposium which is the theme of this book was held at the
Wangaratta Adult Education Centre during the Easter of 1967.
Although the Centre is the ultimate responsibility of the Victorian Education Department, local responsibility for policy-
making and finance has been delegated to the Wangaratta High
School Advisory Council. The citizens of Wangaratta share an
enthusiastic involvement in the Centre's educational aims and, as a
result, the local organizing committee was able to initiate and
successfully carry through such a symposium. Situated in the midst
of the Kelly country as Wangaratta is, this venture caught the
attention of all the major Australian newspapers, attracting resi-
dential students from four states, and culminating in the publication of this book.

# Afterword

> 'I wish to acquaint you with some of the occurrences of
> the present, past and future.'

Did Ned Kelly claim the gift of prophecy when he wrote
those words which open his remarkable Jerilderie letter?
If he did, did he discern that a century after his execution, he would be the subject of song and story? Possibly.
In his public appearances, he chose to speak some
memorable, unforgettable sentences, the stuff of drama
and the seasoning of history.

The very substantial interest aroused not only in Victoria but also throughout Australia by the Kelly Symposium in 1967 reaffirmed the judgement of Russell
Ward in *The Australian Legend* that his name and some of
his fame, or his infamy, had been indelibly imprinted on
the national consciousness: '[E]very child knows something of Ned Kelly'.

Since the publication in 1968 of this book containing
the proceedings of the Symposium, there has been a
steady stream of writing about Kelly and his times, his
trial and his death, his personal qualities and his social
and political significance in Australian history. In 1974
the volume of the *Australian Dictionary of Biography* containing Kelly's entry was published. The late Sir John
Barry, a distinguished member of the same Supreme
Court of Victoria in which Kelly was tried and sentenced,
a critic and a reformer of the penal system, and an
historian as well as a jurist, wrote it. He ended his account
with the estimate that the Kelly legend 'has a compelling
quality that appeals to something deeply rooted in the
character of the "average" Australian'. Kelly has been the
subject of a splendid television play, *The Trial of Ned Kelly*,
by Roger Simpson, which first went to air in September
1977. He and his family have been carefully studied by a
geographer who has as well the insights of a social histo-

rian. John McQuilton's widely acclaimed book *The Kelly Outbreak*, subtitled 'The Geographical Dimension of Social Banditry', published in 1979, canvasses that characterization of Kelly which Ian Jones depicted so vividly for us in Wangaratta: Kelly as rebel, in revolt against specific injustices, 'the pressure and tyrannism of the English yoke'; Kelly striving for the just society (in the Jerilderie letter again):

> I wish those men who joined the stock protection society to withdraw their money and give it and as much more to the widows and orphans and poor of Greta district where I spent and will again spend many a happy day fearless, free and bold . . .

And we have been promised a television series by Ian Jones entitled *The Last Outlaw*, which will be screened, appropriately, in this year, a century after the trial and the execution of Edward Kelly.

So Kelly's memory is not faded but rather refurbished. Of course controversy has not been stilled. In 1978, at Mansfield, the Victoria Police honoured the memory of their fellows who fell at Stringybark Creek a hundred years earlier. In 1980 a petition for a posthumous pardon for Kelly circulates in Victoria.

Perhaps there was second sight in Kelly, a son of Erin. Remember when he stood for sentence before Mr Justice Redmond Barry and said that the day of resolution, 'at a bigger Court than this', was still to come?

LOUIS WALLER
*25 April 1980*

210

# Bibliography

*Cited references*

*Age, The:* Melbourne 1880
  issue 29 October   112, 116, 125–7
  issue 6 November   138
*Argus, The:* Melbourne 1880
  issue 29 October   135–6
  issue 30 October   118–24, 127–8, 134–5, 141
  issue 11 November   101–3
Ashmead, Joseph. 'A True Story of the Kelly Gang'. Unpublished mss   160
*Benalla Standard:* Benalla 1881
  issue 24 April   180
Brown, Max. *Australian Son: The Story of Ned Kelly*   2nd ed., Georgian House: Melbourne 1965   28, 75, 169
*Bulletin:* Sydney 1880
  November issue   12
Byrne, Joe. Letter to Aaron Sherritt dated 26 June 1879; State Archives of Victoria   90–1
  Letter written for Aaron Sherritt from Beechworth Jail: State Archives of Victoria   91
Corfield, Robin. 'The Trial of Ned Kelly'. Unpublished mss   165
Graham, Robert. Letters to Mary Kirk on Kelly gang from Benalla—St. Patrick's Day 1879 to 24 December 1881   86–8
Hare, Police Superintendent. *The Last of the Bushrangers,* London 1895   166
Kelly, Ned. 'Cameron Letter' in Turnbull, Clive (Ed.) *Ned Kelly, Being His Own Story of His Life and Crimes,* Melbourne 1942   13, 134–6
  Jerilderie Letter in Brown, Max *(op. cit.)*   77–80, 81–4, 168
  Statement dictated in Melbourne jail to David Gaunson   98–9
Kenneally, J. J. *Complete Inner History of the Kelly Gang and Their Pursuers,* 7th ed., Robertson and Mullens: Melbourne 1955   158
*Mansfield Guardian:* Mansfield 1879
  July issue   166
O'Hea, Very Rev. Dean. Baptismal Records, St. Paul's Church, Coburg, 1850–70(?)   159

Police File on Ned Kelly now in State Archives of Victoria (Kelly Papers)  174–5

Sadlier, Police Suptd. J.  *Recollections of a Victorian Police Officer*, Melbourne 1913  142, 161, 173, 179, 188

Steele, Police Sgt. Arthur L. M.—see *Legal Documents* below

Turnbull, Clive (Ed.) *Ned Kelly, Being His Own Story of His Life and Crimes*, Melbourne 1942  133–4


### Legal Documents

*Charge for Indictable Offence* (Regina v. Edward Kelly: re murder of Thomas Lonigan)  Facsimile–104; 106

*Notes for Evidence*, Crown Law Department, Melbourne  139, 140, 141, 143

(now in State Archives of Victoria)

*Police Files on Kelly Gang*, State Archives of Victoria (Kelly Papers)  58–9, 141

*Reports of the Royal Commission into the Kelly Outbreak 1881–3* in Parliamentary Papers, Legislative Assembly of Victoria 1881–4  141–2 and see also Index: *Royal Commission*

*Wangaratta Court Record Books*, Wangaratta 1871


### Other References

Barry, Sir John V. 'Edward Kelly' in *Australian Dictionary of Biography*, Vol. V (K-Q, 1851-1890): Melbourne University Press: Melbourne 1974.

Clune, Frank. *The Kelly Hunters*, Angus and Robertson: Sydney 1954 (contains a valuable bibliography)

Clune, Frank (Ed.)  *A Noose For Ned*, Hawthorn Press: Melbourne 1949

Jones, Ian. 'The Years Ned Kelly Went Straight' in *Walkabout*, June 1962

Joy, William and Prior, Tom. *The Bushrangers*, Shakespeare Head Press: Sydney 1963

McQuilton, John. *The Kelly Outbreak*, Melbourne University Press: Melbourne 1979.

Simpson, Roger. *The Trial of Ned Kelly*, Heinemann Educational Australia: Melbourne 1977.

Turnbull, Clive. *Kellyana: A Bibliography of the Kelly Gang*, 1943. (Lists forty-two publications dealing with life and works of Kelly Gang.)

# Index

Thanks are due to the following for their assistance in making available many of the illustrations that appear in this book: The Latrobe Library, Melbourne; The State Archives of Victoria; The Victorian Police Department; Mr. Ian Jones and Mr. Keith McMenomy; Copeland Antiques, St. Kilda.